BEYOND THE BAKE SALE

An Educator's Guide To Working with Parents

By
Anne T. Henderson
Carl L. Marburger
Theodora Ooms

Published by:

The National Committee for Citizens in Education
Suite 410
Wilde Lake Village Green
Columbia, MD 21044

In collaboration with:

The Institute for Educational Leadership
1001 Connecticut Avenue
Washington, DC 20036

The Family Impact Seminar
National Center for Family Studies
Catholic University of America
Washington, DC 20064

Cover Design by Bette Lucey

ISBN 0-934460-27-2
ISBN 0-934460-22-1 Pbk.

Library of Congress Catalog Number 85-61323

Manufactured and printed in the United States of America.

Table of Contents

Foreword

Stop! Do not read *Beyond the Bake Sale* unless you are willing to take a hard look at your beliefs and attitudes about home-school relationships and parent involvement. The authors have some interesting perspectives:

1) A child's education is vitally affected by the quality and character of the relationship between home and school.
2) The current call for school reform and improvement implies that both home and school commit to a stronger and fuller communication effort.
3) Teachers and administrators at local schools must assume the responsibility for initiating and encouraging parental involvement.
4) Effective practices for enhancing parent involvement in schools have been thoroughly researched, and can be replicated in virtually any school setting.

No matter how parents choose the schools their children attend, they need to become actively involved in the life of those schools. Despite what we may hear, choice and involvement are not the same thing. The authors' "challenge to action" is that parents must seek to be involved in what happens to their children in school, and that school staff must nurture that relationship. If a local school's relationship with its families is floundering or unproductive, then a necessary first step is an action plan for change.

If you are open to this exciting challenge, reading *Beyond the Bake Sale* will support and energize your efforts. If, on the other hand, you are dubious, you may be dismayed by the incontrovertible evidence presented for the "parent involvement" case.

My colleagues and I have been actively collaborating with many schools as they work toward school improvement based upon Effective Schools Research. I can testify from this experience that *Beyond the Bake Sale* will greatly assist those committed to the whole of that improvement effort. The authors address the whys and hows of developing positive home/school relations. They know and show that parents can and do make a big difference in promoting the positive characteristics of effective schools.

I believe you will share my view that lasting school improvement will prevail only if we, as educators, pursue and encourage parent involvement and get "Beyond the Bake Sale"!

Lawrence W. Lezotte
Professor of Education Administration
Michigan State University
East Lansing, Michigan

About the Authors

Anne T. Henderson has been an associate with the National Committee for Citizens in Education since 1977, the year her daughter was born. She is the author of *The Evidence Grows*, an annotated bibliography showing the positive relationship between parent involvement and student achievement, and several other NCCE reports and publications. In addition, she has represented the interests and concerns of parents and citizens before Congress and federal agencies.

Carl L. Marburger is one of three Senior Associates at the National Committee for Citizens in Education, which was founded in 1973. He is a parent and has been a public school teacher and administrator. Just before coming to NCCE, he was Commissioner of Education for the State of New Jersey.

He is the author of many books and publications, including *Who Controls the Schools?*, a handbook on the political realities of education governance, and most recently, *One School at a Time: School Based Management, A Process for Change*, a book on how to bring democratic decision making to our schools.

Theodora Ooms, M.S.W., has been with the Family Impact Seminar since 1976 and became the Director in 1982. From 1982-1983 she directed the Seminar's *Families and Schools Project*. Prior to coming to Washington she worked directly with families and children as a social worker and family therapist. She has extensive experience collaborating with school personnel and was Coordinator of Consultation and Education at the Philadelphia Child Guidance Clinic. Her special interest in schools grows both from her professional experiences and from being a parent of three children.

She edited the book, *Teenage Pregnancy in a Family*

Context: Implications for Policy (1981), and has authored numerous reports and articles.

Acknowledgments

This book is the joint effort of the National Committee for Citizens in Education, the Family Impact Seminar, and the Institute for Educational Leadership. We wish to thank the NCCE staff for all their encouragement and support: Stan Salett, Bill Rioux, Chrissie Bamber, and Nancy Berla for their advice and enthusiasm; Lynn Holmes, Pat Fort, Maryanne Blair, Jackie Mosberg, Janet Gosnell, and Mia Darbouze for their superb logistical and production efforts.

There were also all those who graciously agreed to read and comment on our draft manuscript, which was much revised to incorporate their concerns and suggestions: Patricia Bauch, Lee Greene, Cynthia Dubea, David Imig, Mary Eno Wagner, Mary Lynch Barnds, Steven Redfield, Betty Felton, Bonnie Doubert, Bill Rosenbloom, Tom Koerner, Beverly Harad, and Dale Berlin.

This book draws on the findings of the Family Impact Seminar's *Families and Schools Project*, which was conducted in collaboration with the Colorado Congress of Parents, Teachers & Students and the Connecticut League of Women Voters, at the time that the Seminar was based at the Institute for Educational Leadership. The FIS wishes to thank all those involved both as advisors to the project and as participants in the invitational working conference held in January, 1983. We hope they find their many insights and experiences reflected in these pages. The authors, of course, take full responsibility for their contents.

Most especially, the FIS wants to thank project staff and consultants Elizabeth Bode, Darlene Craddock, Susan Farkas, Ruth Hubbell, Susan Ginsberg, Sheila Kraft, Nina Parker-Cohen, Marcia Levine, Heather Weiss and Sheri Williams for their hard work and many insights. We thank Sidney Johnson (former Seminar Director), Mike Usdan, Ray Valdivieso, Lisa Walker and Mildred Garcia of the Institute for Educational Leadership for their encouragement and support from beginning to end. Our gratitude also goes to Jim Comer, Don Davies, Oliver Moles, David Seeley and Mark Shedd to whom we often turned for insights, advice and assistance, and to many people in the Connecticut and Colorado State Departments of Education, the school principals and staff and the Urban League of Greater New Haven who greatly facilitated the study.

Our special appreciation is extended to our collaborating teams in Connecticut and Colorado for their time, energy, enthusiasm and persistence in conducting the interviews and observations which tapped the experience of parents and educators: *Colorado PTA*—Marti Ahlenius (State Coordinator), Vera Faulkner (President), and Sheila Cesario, Muriel Green, Carol Naff, Pamela Neelan, Sheri Williams (District Coordinators); and *Connecticut League of Women Voters*—Laurie Hart Docknevich (State Coordinator), Percy Langstaff (President), Marlene Wenograd (Vice President), and Selene Bennett, Betsy Ratner, Sandy Scheraga (District Coordinators) and numerous volunteer interviewers in each state.

The *Families and Schools Project* was funded by grants from the Charles Stewart Mott Foundation and the Ford Foundation. We are most grateful to the project officers, Marilyn Steele (Mott) and Edward Meade (Ford) for all of their encouragement, support and patience while waiting for this final product.

The authors wish also to thank the National Coalition for Parent Involvement in Education (NCPIE) for its grant to publicize the book, and for the special marketing arrangements made to distribute the book to members of NCPIE organizations. NCPIE is a coalition of organizations that support parent involvement in education.

About the Publishers

The National Committee for Citizens in Education

NCCE is a private, non-profit organization devoted exclusively to improving the quality of public schools through increased public involvement. Through its information resources, which include a toll-free hot line, a series of jargon-free handbooks and films, and a training program, NCCE provides the information resources parents and citizens need to become involved in education decisions at the local level. NCCE also offers School Based Management training to help parents and educators to work constructively together.

The Institute for Educational Leadership

The Institute for Educational Leadership, Inc. is a non-profit organization headquartered in Washington, D.C. which serves policymakers in education, government and business in a non-partisan fashion as they make decisions affecting education. Established in 1971, IEL's work combines leadership development, networking and convening, and providing neutral ground and information for policy discussion. The Institute has developed and supported diverse programs, including: the Education Policy Fellowship Program, State Education Policy Seminars in conjunction with the Education Commission of the States, Fellows in Educational Journalism, Work/Education Fellowship Program, Superintendent's Roundtable, Education Issues Team, and MetroLink. In addition, IEL is associated with the Hispanic Policy Development Project.

The Family Impact Seminar

The Family Impact Seminar, established in 1976 at the

Institute for Educational Leadership, aims to encourage a family perspective in the development, implementation, and evaluation of policy. It conducts family impact studies, convenes conferences and seminars, and provides information and technical assistance. Through these various activities the Seminar hopes to encourage the exchange of knowledge between scholars, human service professionals, and policymakers. The Seminar is especially interested in the implications of changing family patterns on a wide range of human services and in identifying needed changes in policy and practice that would be more supportive of family life. In 1982 the Seminar joined the National Center for Family Studies, the Catholic University of America, to become its non-partisan, non-sectarian policy research and analysis unit.

Introduction

The evidence is clear. When parents are involved in children's schooling, children do better in school and they go to better schools. Both families and schools want the best for children: they want to help them learn, grow, and develop into educated, responsible, and caring adults. Because they share the same basic goals, it seems obvious that parents and educators should be working together.

If asked, most parents, teachers, and principals will agree that parents need to be involved in and supportive of education. Yet in many places, parents are not actively involved in the life of the school; instead they are spending most of their time and energies organizing bake sales, if they are involved at all.

All too often, families and schools seem to be "worlds apart"—distant and independent, barely communicating with each other, or hostile and at war, giving contradictory messages to each other and to the child who is caught between them. Clearly, we must find ways of helping schools and parents work together for the sake of our children.

We feel it is particularly timely to take a fresh look at the relations between families and schools, because we have all become acutely aware of the tremendous changes in family life that have taken place in the last twenty years. We all know that the traditional nuclear family, in which most of us grew up, where two parents are married to each other and living together, the father the breadwinner and the mother the homemaker, is no longer the dominant model. In fact, the family structures and cultural backgrounds of children in school seem to be becoming ever more diverse and complex.

Educators are understandably uneasy and perplexed about what these changes mean for children, for parents, and for the schools they are expected to run. Current statistics give an idea of their magnitude:

- One out of two marriages ends in divorce.
- Half of all children can expect to spend some time living with only one parent before they are eighteen.
- One in five adolescent girls can expect to become pregnant before she leaves high school.
- The majority of school-aged children have mothers in the work force.

These trends vastly complicate matters for educators. How can we stimulate more parent involvement if mothers work outside the home? Which parents do we try to reach, the stepparent a child lives with or the father who lives across town; the kindergartner's 34-year-old grandmother or 19-year-old mother? What responsibility do we have to help children cope with the stress of their parents' breaking up? How can we ask overburdened single parents to help teachers educate their children? How can we be adequately sensitive to cultural, social, and economic differences, and collaborate with parents who cannot speak English or whose cultural background makes our way of thinking and doing things almost incomprehensible?

In spite of these and myriad other difficulties that family-school partnerships may entail, working together is critically important for students. It is surprising that all the recent blue-ribbon reports on education reform and improvement almost totally neglected this issue. Through this handbook, we hope to provide some constructive and encouraging advice:

- To help build trust and confidence between parents and educators.
- To describe the different roles parents play in and around school.
- To provide teachers and principals with some compelling reasons for involving parents.
- To suggest many specific ways parents can be con-

structively involved and to recommend some ways to proceed.

- To offer a checklist for gauging your school's current strengths and liabilities.
- To suggest changes in district, state, and federal policies that will facilitate stronger home-school collaboration.
- To present an up-to-date synthesis of what the research is saying about family-school partnerships.

Who Should Read This Guide?

This book is addressed primarily to those people on the firing line who deal daily with the unique issues and problems of the school, and with parents, families, and communities. It is for those principals and teachers who most need information and suggestions about effective ways to build partnerships between schools and the families of the neighborhood.

Another important audience is state and local boards of education members, supervisors, and their staffs, who set the tone for a district and create the policy framework within which collaboration with families takes place.

An additional audience is the faculty of colleges and graduate schools who train prospective teachers and administrators, as well as those who provide in-service education experiences for educators. What we hear from large numbers of teachers and administrators is that there is little or no available training in ways to work with parents and families. We hope that this guide will prove useful to college and university personnel concerned about this often neglected aspect of training public school personnel.

We also hope that some parents, citizens, and students—all those concerned about the quality of public schooling—will find this handbook helpful. They can play a most useful role in bringing these ideas to the attention of educators and policy makers, and in advocating necessary changes.

While most of the work we draw from has focused on public schools, we also hope this guide will be useful to educators working in schools that are not publicly funded, including parochial or religiously sponsored, and non-sectarian independent schools. Many of the needs are the same, and the interest is there.

With each of these constituencies in mind, this handbook has sections designed to inform, encourage, and provoke, as well as sections that can be used over and over again in school improvement efforts. It describes the various ways parents can be involved in the schools, and how educators need to examine their own attitudes before they can work effectively with parents. It also includes a framework for building a home-school partnership, with step-by-step information on how to build parent involvement; barriers to and helpful hints for establishing successful partnerships; and checklists that will be invaluable tools in your school improvement process. Finally, we offer conclusions and recommendations that will help educators take the lead in creating a partnership with families and others who are concerned about the quality of education in their community.

Clarification of Terms: We would like to make a distinction between "participation" and "involvement." Dictionaries offer some guidance:

Participate: to enjoy, or suffer with others; to have a share in common with others.

Involve: to cause to be inextricably associated or concerned; to engross or occupy absorbingly.

There is a difference! That difference might best be described by modifying the old story of the chicken and the pig. As they walked past a restaurant, they noticed a sign saying, "Breakfast: Ham and Eggs—$2.50." The chicken said, "I'll have you know that I participated in creating that breakfast." The pig replied, "For me it was total involvement."

Perhaps it really doesn't matter what we call it. It only matters that the commitment, the energy, and the enthusiasm are there. If school staff honestly want parents and citizens to be a part of the school experience, if they are willing to make the commitment in time and energy because they believe it is important, then children will benefit.

So, because it implies that sense of commitment, we shall use the word "involvement" here to describe the ways parents and citizens can and should participate in school activities.

Another clarification also seems necessary at this point. You may have noticed that we occasionally use "parents" and "citizens" to describe those who can potentially be involved in schools. We believe it is important to use both those terms in describing possible participants in school activities.

• "Parents" are those with legal or quasi-legal custodianship, whether biological, adoptive, or foster parents of the child who attends a particular school. This term also includes other family members (uncles, sisters, grandparents) whose involvement may be important to the child.

• "Citizens" are the residents of the community who do not currently have children in school. They may be senior citizens, business people, labor union members, shop owners, or landlords, but they may all become involved in the affairs of the public school. And they are most important to the school. They can often provide objective and more dispassionate points of view. They can support the school through their individual contribution and expertise. And they can help pass (or at least not work to defeat) bond, budget, or millage proposals. Most of them either have had or will have the experience of being parents. Many are grandparents. (One exception is the parents of private school children. It is most important to involve these citizens in the operation of the public schools, as well.)

• "Parent-teacher organizations" is the general term we

use to refer to a variety of parent groups with different names and structures organized around the school. Some are called "PTA" (and may be affiliated with the national Parent Teacher Association), others may be called "PTO," "Home and School Association," or "Parent Council." These organizations define their roles quite differently from school to school and carry out a varied range of activities, from bake sales to school management.

● "Secondary schools" is the term we use to cover the range of school organizations that cover grades 7-12 and, occasionally, grades 5 and 6; they may be middle, junior high, or senior high schools.

An additional statement needs to be made here. We wish to make clear that when we use the term "school," we mean a special learning environment, no two of which are exactly alike. While there may be similarities in curriculum, each school has a unique size, setting, pupil population, community, faculty, and climate; and any description of family-school relations must be flexible enough to encompass that diversity.

Further, although the research and practice has generally focused on the relationship between the family and elementary schools, we shall also examine these issues at the secondary school level.

Creating a successful family-school partnership is a difficult process. Most parents are ready and willing to become involved in such a partnership if they had more encouragement from the school staff. Principals and teachers might wonder, "Will involving parents make my job more effective, more workable? When I am feeling besieged and the schools are being 'dumped on' by nearly everyone, will the extra energy and time needed make a difference for children?"

Our answer is, "YES!"

A Note About Style: While the ideas and examples we present are based on a considerable body of research and experience, we decided we did not want this guide to resemble a research paper. Thus, we have not footnoted or (usually) quoted references in the text. Instead, we include in an "Afterword" a summary review of the research, and a selected bibliography and list of relevant organizations in the "Appendices."

CHAPTER 1
Five Types
of Parent Involvement

What Do We Mean by "Parent Involvement"?

Many educators say they are strongly in favor of parent involvement, yet it is not at all clear what they mean by the term. Most are probably referring to parents' participation in home-school activities—such as bake sales and fairs—to raise funds for the band uniforms or school computer, or they may mean parents helping in the classroom or on school trips. Some may be referring to special programs designed to encourage parents of young children to become more involved with their children in learning activities at home.

Other educators feel less positive about parent involvement, thinking instead about incidents where parents have insisted that certain books be banned from the school library, particular courses not be taught, or a teacher be fired.

Yet others are ambivalent about parent involvement, thinking about "Back-to-School" nights or parent-teacher conferences, which on some occasions turn out to be useful and constructive, but on others are boring rituals or even quite hostile encounters.

"Parent involvement," therefore, is a broad and loosely defined term. In spite of much official rhetoric in its favor, parent involvement is not always regarded favorably by school personnel.

In this guide, we argue unequivocally that educators should strengthen the family-school relationship by encouraging and nurturing parent involvement. We do, however, understand the reasons for hesitation and uncertainty. Before we discuss these, we need first to clarify the various kinds of roles that parents may play with regard to their children's education. We have grouped the activities in which parents take part into five basic roles (Several others have made similar distinctions. See references: Williams and Stallworth, 1983/4; Collins et al., 1982).

Parent Roles in Education

1. Partners: Parents performing basic obligations for their child's education and social development.

2. Collaborators and Problem Solvers: Parents reinforcing the school's efforts with their child and helping to solve problems.

3. Audience: Parents attending and appreciating the school's (and their child's) performance and productions.

4. Supporters: Parents providing volunteer assistance to teachers, the parent organization, and to other parents.

5. Advisors and/or Co-decision Makers: Parents providing input on school policy and program though membership in ad hoc or permanent governance bodies.

We will now discuss these roles in more detail, providing examples of the types of activities that exemplify each role.

Role 1: Parents as Partners

From the moment of birth, parents and other family members are the child's first and primary educators. Indeed, children learn how to talk and use language skills at home. They also learn values and social skills from their families. While this responsibility does not end once their child enters kindergarten, the responsibility must now be shared with professional educators. Parents continue to teach their children a great deal, but now they also have to carry out a number of obligations relating to their partner,

3

the school.

We tend to forget how much parents do to make it possible for educators to teach their children. Parents register their child and ensure that he or she is properly dressed, gets to school on time, and attends each day. They purchase necessary supplies and equipment, and obtain the required vaccinations and medical exams. Parents are expected to read, and often respond to, written communications from the school about schedules, procedures, special events, and policies. They are frequently asked to sign and return permission and information forms and report cards. They are expected to respond to phone calls and notes from the teacher. In some schools (though this seems to be the exception), all parents are required to attend a parent-teacher conference at least once a year. (In parochial or other private schools, even more is usually required of parents—for example, paying fees, buying uniforms and books, and contributing substantial amounts of volunteer time or resources.)

Most of these tasks are a direct consequence of parents' legal responsibility to enroll their child in school. Accompanying this responsibility are corresponding parental rights, also established by law: access to school records, due process in disciplinary procedures, and participation in the decisions regarding placement in special education programs.

These regular activities and contacts between parents and schools are the core of the family-school relationship. Educators tend to forget that it's not easy for parents to carry out these tasks faithfully and promptly, especially when they have several children often attending different schools, and when both are often employed.

Although this type of parent involvement is engaged in by almost all parents, it is the least often noted and discussed. Taking a critical look at the current state of parent-school communication concerning the basic responsibilities just discussed may have the greatest potential for strengthening the family-school partnership.

Role 2: Parents as Collaborators and Problem Solvers

Research has indicated that positive parent involvement plays a large role in determining whether children do well in school. Parents can encourage and reward satisfactory achievement and behavior and show interest in what happens during the school day. Parents demonstrate how important they believe school is by their reaction to absences, minor illnesses, and truancy; their policies on bedtime and television; and whether they help their child complete homework.

Parents can also stimulate and reinforce learning by providing a variety of enrichment activities: reading to their young child, taking trips to the museums and library, discussing possible careers, and demonstrating their own interest and curiosity in the world around them. Experiments with early childhood programs such as Headstart, where parents are heavily involved and trained in ways to help their children learn, have often been very successful.

A major aspect of the parent's role as effective collaborator is its potential to help school personnel resolve problems that may arise with a child's learning or behavior. When a child is falling behind in schoolwork, having difficulty with peers, acting withdrawn, or being disruptive, teachers naturally need to understand the nature of the problem and figure out what to do about it. The "cause" can be a single factor—a "disability" in the child or the wrong class placement—or a combination of factors, such as distress in the family, too permissive a teacher, and conflicting expectations between parents and teacher. But research and clinical experience suggests that the problem can rarely be adequately understood or resolved without involving the child's family.

Parents need to be promptly alerted to the difficulty and called in as consultants to figure out, with the teacher, what to do about the problem. Often a strategy can then be developed that may involve changes in the behavior of the

5

teacher, parent, and child. And when this is not sufficient, the school's role is to work out a plan with the parent for getting additional help within the school or from outside resources.

This problem-solving process is often not as smooth as just outlined. In fact, a good deal of mutual blaming and conflict may erupt between parent and teacher, and considerable negotiation and mediation skills may be required of a third party (counselor, principal, or outside consultant).

Schools need to examine carefully whether their current policies and practices facilitate or hinder parent involvement in effective problem solving. Many surveys have voiced parents' complaints that they hear from school only when something goes wrong, and often much too late.

Developing successful problem-solving practices that involve parents as collaborators can improve school achievement and behavior for the child, prevent some of the need for special education placement, and create more orderly classrooms. Studies show that this role is much neglected by schools.

Role 3: Parents as Audience

The first two roles we have just described can be fulfilled by parents essentially from their home base. Only occasionally is their presence needed in the school building. However, schools also sponsor several activities and events designed to draw parents into the school.

Most elementary and many secondary schools hold "open houses" during the day, or "Back-to-School" nights once a year, often under the auspices of the parent-teacher organization. In addition, most schools invite parents to concerts, plays, exhibitions, and athletic events. These are highly visible steps toward bridging the gap between families and schools. The parents' role on these occasions, however, is largely a passive one. They are to listen, observe, applaud, and occasionally ask questions.

6

These events are designed primarily to provide parents with information about the school faculty and staff. When substantial numbers of parents attend, the school gains by feeling their support and interest in the school community as a whole. Parents gain from acquiring a more direct, personal knowledge of the school. Especially at the younger grades (but even through high school), children usually feel good about their parents' showing interest in the place where, and people with whom, they spend so much of each weekday.

The level of parent participation in these school-sponsored activities varies from school to school and family to family. It is much less likely that low-income, minority, or non-English speaking parents participate in these events, especially if they are a small minority of parents in the school. There are many reasons for this. Among them may be distance from the school, lack of transportation, difficulty in finding babysitters for the other children, and uneasiness in a physical and cultural environment that seems strange or forbidding. Yet these are the very parents that school personnel need to help feel comfortable and familiar with the school, so they can support their child's adjustment and progress.

Role 4: Parents as Supporters

In American public and private schools, there is a strong tradition of parents providing a wide range of volunteer assistance, both to their own children's teachers and to the school as a whole. Parents (usually mothers, although there are an increasing number of fathers) may serve as "room parents" in elementary schools, organizing help through "telephone trees" to obtain needed supplies or assistance with school trips, or to deal with emergencies. Parents volunteer in school libraries, provide tutoring to children in special need, make attendance calls, or share their special expertise in enrichment programs. Parents organized as a

7

group (sometimes affiliated with the National PTA, or as an independent parent association) may sponsor many of these volunteer activities, or they can be sponsored by a local unit of the National School Volunteer Program, which brings in parents and citizens from the community to help in the school.

In addition, parent-teacher organizations have traditionally played a big role in sponsoring fund-raising events, such as bazaars, fairs, and auctions, which support the school by paying for special equipment or programs that are not in the school's budget.

Although only small numbers of parents commit much time and energy to these volunteer activities, a large number of parents and their children benefit from them.

Parents help other parents in a variety of ways. In today's mobile and often impersonal communities, parents quickly discover that they welcome information, advice, and various kinds of practical help from other parents to assist them in raising their children and cooperating with the school. The parent-teacher organization frequently publishes address lists and regular newsletters and sponsors parent education programs—talks, workshops, seminars—to help parents improve their understanding of child development and learn better ways of handling their children.

Less formally, parents create carpools that allow their children to participate in extracurricular activities, or take turns caring for younger children after school. Less traditional forms of assistance are emerging in response to new parental needs. In some communities, parents have been resourceful in responding to needs for preschool and school-age child care. Urban safety issues have resulted in designated "Safe Block" homes where a parent is present for refuge or on sudden dismissal, such as snow days. The large number of "latchkey" children have stimulated parent-organized "hot lines" that children in difficulty can call. In some communities, parents have become sensitive to the difficulties of non-English speaking families and developed hospitality committees or host families.

Parents of junior-high and senior-high students, sharing a growing alarm about the problems of drug and alcohol abuse and drunk driving, have organized in various kinds of support and action groups, both to develop preventive efforts and to provide assistance to those whose children are experiencing the problem. Some of these efforts have taken on the dimensions of a national movement, such as MADD and SADD (Mothers/Students Against Drunk Driving). Because parents of high-school students in many communities frequently do not know each other, parent peer groups are forming in an attempt to create a more cohesive social structure and develop some common guidelines for parties and curfews.

In the area of special education, some districts have programs in which parents may volunteer and receive training to be parent advocates. They accompany a nervous parent of a handicapped child through the regular processes of special education diagnosis and placement. When necessary, this parent advocate may accompany the parent through the due process procedures if the parent appeals a decision about placement, diagnosis, or prescribed treatment.

Finally, parent support networks can provide invaluable assistance in especially stressful situations when, for example, a mother dies or is seriously ill, when a chronically sick child undergoes many hospitalizations, or when a family is rendered homeless after a fire.

It is important that educators recognize the value of these parent-to-parent activities, and encourage them as much as they can, for they indirectly help further the goals of the school.

Role 5: Parents as Advisors and Co-decision Makers

In response to increasing dissatisfaction with the remoteness of large, centralized school bureaucracies, school systems in various parts of the country have been experimenting with ways to obtain advice from parents and citizens, or to give them a share in policy decisions. Perhaps the most common approach is for a principal to name special committees of parent and teacher representatives to work out solutions to a schoolwide problem, such as discipline or safety, or to help introduce a new program or curriculum, such as a sex education unit.

In some school districts, state-mandated school accountability committees or advisory councils function as monitoring or advisory bodies. These groups sometimes serve a perfunctory role, approving a bland year-end report; but at other times they can play a crucial role, as in selecting a new principal, creating a new discipline policy, or conducting a school-wide needs assessment. Real power-sharing with parents occurs when parents become elected to school governing boards or are equal members on "school site councils," consisting of representatives from the teachers, parents, and administrators, which make decisions about the expenditure of discretionary school funds. In some private schools parents wield decisive power through being a majority of the governing board.

The federal government has played an important role in encouraging strong individual and group parental input in school decision making. In P.L. 94-142, the Education for All Handicapped Children Act of 1975, Congress required that parents be involved in special education placement decisions. And through the late 1960's and 1970's, Congress enacted and amended four federal compensatory and bilingual education programs for the disadvantaged which mandated parent advisory committees—Headstart, Follow-Through, Title I, and the Bilingual Education Act. (In 1981, Congress repealed the parent involvement provision in Title I, at the request of the Reagan Administration. Other proposals to repeal parent advisory roles were not successful.)

The number of parents who serve in these advisory and decision-making roles is small, and it can be difficult to ascertain how well they represent the views of the parent body. Procedures for their appointment or election may not be particularly democratic, nor may there be clearly marked channels for them to communicate with parents as a whole. Also, parent training is frequently necessary for parent input to be real and not token. Yet if it is made very clear to parents on which issues their advice is needed and

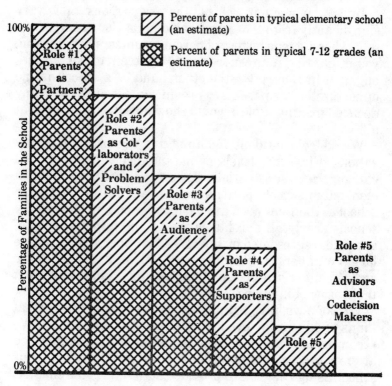

Diagram A
Five Types of Parent Involvement*

*Note: The proportions presented in this diagram are based on experience, not research.

which decisions are negotiable, parents can play a useful and helpful role in governance of schools.

A Parent Involvement Profile

Diagram A, "Five Types of Parent Involvement," presents a parent involvement profile for two typical schools. The height of each column shows the approximate proportion of parents in the school that engage in each type of role. The bold line represents the proportion for the elementary school, the dotted line for the upper-grades school.

In any particular school, the proportions may vary significantly from those illustrated here. For example, if a school has a strong history of parent volunteer participation, you might find many more than 50 percent of the families engaged in Role 4. On the other hand, if a school has no opportunities for parents to provide advice or share in any decision making, Role 5 would show no parents involved at all.

We do feel confident about making two broad generalizations. First, the levels of parent involvement in each category are substantially lower in secondary than in elementary schools; parents tend to become less involved in school as their children grow older. Second, in elementary schools nearly all parents carry out the minimal level of activities represented by Role 1. In the upper grades, where larger numbers of students have problems with attendance or drop out of school, many parents may fail to carry out their basic obligations.

We hope we have stimulated your curiosity about what kinds of parent involvement you have in your school. We recommend that, after reading through this chapter, you attempt to construct a profile of parent involvement in your school, using Diagram B provided at the end of the chapter.

Which Roles Are Most Important?

We have identified five distinct roles that parents play with regard to their children's schooling. Roles 1, 2, and 3 involve parents in activities that benefit their own child, Roles 4 and 5 largely benefit the school as a whole, with benefits accruing only *indirectly* to the parents' own child. This distinction is important because it may help to explain why so few parents are active in these last two roles, when it is less clear that their involvement will benefit their own child.

Faced with so many types of parent involvement, a parent, teacher, or principal might well ask, "Which are more important? I can't do or encourage them all!" If the issue is which kinds of parent involvement have the most immediate "payoff" in terms of student achievement, the first and second roles are probably the most directly important ones to work on. If the question is, "How can I, as principal, boost the image of my school in the community, or stretch my limited resources further, build a stronger school program, or help defuse the lack of trust and confidence of the community in the school?" the answer is to encourage more parent participation in the fourth and fifth roles.

Another important issue is whether and how these different kinds of parent involvement are linked. If a few parents are actively involved in advisory and governance roles, will all parents in the school be more likely to build strong collaborative relationships with teachers? If parents provide large amounts of volunteer assistance to the school, will school personnel be more likely to welcome their input on advisory committees?

We do not have any hard evidence to answer these important questions. There is some indication that in "effective schools," where the principal and faculty have a strong commitment to working in partnership with parents, all these types of parent involvement flourish and reinforce each other. In other schools, without such a commitment,

13

some types of parent involvement may be strong and others largely missing, due to the particular history of the school, federal mandates, or the specific energies and interests of

---

Diagram B
Construct a Profile
of Parent Involvement in Your School

Instructions: For each type of involvement, estimate the percent of families who participate. Draw a line across each column to construct your school's profile.

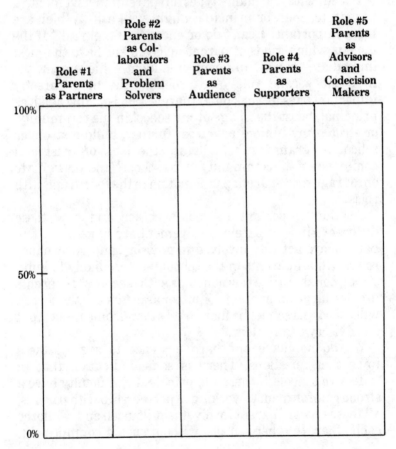

Role #1 Parents as Partners | Role #2 Parents as Collaborators and Problem Solvers | Role #3 Parents as Audience | Role #4 Parents as Supporters | Role #5 Parents as Advisors and Codecision Makers

100%
50%
0%

particular teachers or parents. Some schools may have very active parent-educator councils, for example, yet these councils may have never addressed the issue of improving communication and collaboration between parents and teachers at the classroom level.

We will return to this question about how you can decide your school's priorities for parent involvement later, in Chapter 7.

Exercise 1: What Is Your School's Parent Involvement Profile?

Now that we have finished this review of the five types of parent involvement, turn to Diagram B and try filling out the chart to construct a parent involvement profile of your own school. Because you may not be able to find any hard data within the school on which to base this profile, we suggest that you do this exercise with a small team—a key teacher, the office secretary, and the president of your parent organization or some other active parent—who can help you with your estimates.

CHAPTER 2

Basic Assumptions: What Do You Think?

Families and schools need to interlock in a cooperative way that encourages the child's learning and maturing as a social being. Children must not experience family and school as worlds apart, nor find themselves in the battle zone between two warring factions.

The purpose of this chapter is to probe a bit into educators' attitudes about parent involvement, to explore assumptions, beliefs, and practices. Understanding attitudes is an important first step toward working more effectively with parents.

Many educators are on the record for parent involvement, but does the rhetoric match with the reality? How much parent involvement could you feel comfortable with in your school? Which of the roles that parents play (as described in Chapter 1) do you feel are helpful? Which roles do you think are obstructive? Are your attitudes about parents consistent with your educational philosophy? Have they varied in different settings?

The assumptions educators make run along a continuum— at one end there are those who say that schools can be effective without any parent involvement; at the other, there are those who feel that schools cannot be effective without close collaboration with parents.

In the next few pages, we have placed the attitudes which belong to the more formal, "professionals only" approach (labeled "Set A") alongside the attitudes we associate with the more open-ended, collaborative approach (labeled "Set B"). We do not expect that anyone would totally identify with one side or the other, but we hope this will give you some insight into your thinking patterns, and how those in your school might feel.

17

Exercise 2: Examining Your Attitudes About Parent Involvement

These statements are paired. Place a "check" beside the one which most closely corresponds to your own attitude and beliefs.

Set A

1. Home and school are separate, very different worlds. It is the school's responsibility to educate children, and the parent's responsibility to see that the children are dressed, fed, and prepared for school.

2. Educators are trained professionals whose job is to teach children; the expertise of most parents is in other areas.

3. The most effective school organizational structure is one where decisions are made by the principal and carried out by teachers and staff.

4. Parents should cooperate with school policies and procedures, and should be active in providing general program support. Their primary role is to reinforce the school's efforts at home.

5. Parents have no place in educational decisions about school management, curriculum, or staffing. They delegate these tasks to educators.

6. When a child is having a learning problem in school, school personnel, including specialists, should investigate the nature of the child's problem. If it is serious, they should then inform the parents about their recommendations, and of any need for referral to outside specialists.

Set B

1. Schools share the responsibility for education with parents. The partnership with parents is flexible: on some issues the parents will be the more active partner; on others the school will be.

2. Educators and parents have complementary expertise about educating children which should be mutually respected and used.

3. Educators should work as collaborative teams with each other and with parents. Where possible, decisions should be reached by a consensus.

4. Parents should be involved actively, both in helping their children and in supporting the school program as a whole. Parents should be offered a wide range of oppportunities to be involved, at home and at school.

5. Many educational decisions (even about curriculum and staffing) should be made with some input from parents.

6. When a child is having a learning problem, the school should consult promptly with the parents in a joint effort to understand the nature of the difficulty and to plan strategies to resolve it.

Set A

7. The problems most children have in school are based on their own character and personality and/or the home environment.

8. Every effort should be made to resolve school-wide problems using existing structures within the school system. If the teacher and the principal are unable to resolve a problem, they should turn to their administrative superiors in the district office.

9. Involving parents or the local community in solving a school problem will undermine local support for the school and damage its reputation.

10. Schools should not get involved in private family problems of divorce, teen pregnancy, maternal employment, or drug abuse. Nor should a school be expected to meet the problems of minority, foreign, or immigrant families. A school's function is to educate children, not babysit, counsel, or provide services for their families.

11. The needs and convenience of the school system should have first priority in determining the school schedule, calendar, and special events. Parents should make every effort to attend conferences and meetings at the times scheduled.

12. Parents have a number of tasks to perform to carry out their basic legal responsibilities. When parents do not fulfill these, we have to assume they are uncooperative and/or apathetic about their child's education.

13. It is the teacher's job to provide information about school curriculum and their child's progress to parents. Most parents have little to contribute in this area, as they are not educators or experts in child development.

Set B

7. The problems children have are the product of interaction between the child, the school setting, and the home; no one person or factor is usually "to blame."

8. When a school-wide problem arises the teachers and principal should try at the outset to involve every sector affected, including parents, students, administrators, and the community.

9. Many school-wide problems cannot be resolved without community support and cooperation.

10. Recognizing that children's family problems can seriously impair their education, the school should assume some responsibility to respond to the special needs of working parents, divorced or separated parents, and minority or immigrant families.

11. In determining the school schedule, calendar and special events, the school should recognize the constraints on parents who are tied to rigid work schedules, long hours, and job sites far from home. It should consciously strive to find a balance among the needs of today's families, school personnel, and organizational efficiency.

12. Parents have a number of tasks to perform to carry out their basic legal responsibilities, but when parents fail to perform them, the school should try to help parents do so.

13. Teachers should create channels for two-way communication with parents; they should encourage parents to raise questions, share their knowledge of their child, and express their expectations and concerns.

Set A

14. Most parents are comfortable with leaving their children's education to skilled professional educators and do not want to intrude in school affairs.

15. Parents should be informed of any serious behavior problems their child has after school personnel have decided on a diagnosis and recommendations.

16. The school should not be expected to make special efforts to encourage parent attendance at special events, or to organize activities for parents unrelated to the school program.

17. Only a few parents want to be very active in providing volunteer assistance to the school program.

18. Parents (or parent organizations) should provide basic information to other parents through newsletters, address lists, and educational meetings, but need not generally provide other supportive services to parents.

19. It is rarely appropriate for parents to provide input into program or policy decisions, or to help solve schoolwide problems.

20. It is accepted that parents have the right to express their dissatisfactions through regular administrative channels (first to the principal, then to the district or school board).

_____ TOTAL NUMBER OF CHECKS IN SET A.

Set B

14. Most parents want to be actively involved in their children's education. This interest should be welcomed and encouraged by the school.

15. Parents should be consulted when the school first becomes concerned about their child's behavior, and should be actively involved in developing strategies to deal with the problem.

16. When certain groups of parents do not participate in school events, the school should develop creative ways, with other parents' help, to overcome barriers to their participation.

17. The school should offer a wide range of volunteer activities for parents which make best use of their varied skills, resources, and time, and should expect each family to contribute some time to the school.

18. The parent organization should provide a newsletter, address lists, and educational programs to help parents. In addition, it should be alert to the special needs of some groups of families, such as those headed by single parents, and develop programs to meet these needs.

19. Parents should be offered a variety of ways to provide input into program and policy decisions and help resolve schoolwide problems.

20. The principal should provide clear guidelines to parents about which decisions are open for negotiation and shared decision-making, and which are not.

————— TOTAL NUMBER OF CHECKS IN SET B

What Do Your Answers Mean?

We recognize that many educators with attitudes that fall at the formal end of the spectrum (Set A) have provided excellent educational experience for children. While the research clearly shows that parent involvement improves student achievement, it also has documented some effective schools that have little or no parent involvement.

A purely formal approach to education seems to work best when there is a stable community and a congruity of values between home and school. It assumes "traditional" two-parent families with the mother working at home; that school personnel come from backgrounds similar to their students; and that the staff have the respect, trust, and understanding of parents. In this setting, it can be perfectly appropriate for parents to delegate the responsibility for education to the professionals. Few schools in the public sector can make any of these assumptions today.

The collaborative approach (Set B), which we support, not only recognizes that schools cannot cope alone with the tremendous changes in society, but also draws on a rich understanding of how important the family's role is in education.

We suggest that you might look now at the statements in Exercise 2 where you found you wanted to check both pairs. This may indicate an area of tension or conflict, or it may mean you are in the middle of the two positions. In this case, try re-wording one of the sentences so that it more closely resembles your opinion.

Then, look at the items where you checked neither Set A nor Set B. This, too, could be a trouble spot. Is there a mid-way point between the two where you would be comfortable? If you cannot resolve the problem easily, we recommend that you finish this book, then return to this chapter and go through the exercise again. Have you moved? Are you willing to re-examine your attitudes?

How can schools learn to work more effectively with parents? Understanding your attitudes is only a first step.

In the next two chapters we will provide some positive practices and guidelines that should be directly helpful to you, and lay out a step-by-step process for building parent involvement.

CHAPTER 3

Developing a Family-School Partnership in Every School

T here is no blueprint for "The Partnership School"— the school that collaborates effectively with parents. Because schools are so different, there is no single model, no one set of practices or characteristics, to which we can point and say, "Aha! That is the definitive Partnership School." But all schools that work well with parents share a fundamental set of principles. If the principal, school staff, and parents do not subscribe to most of these principles, their attempts to increase parent involvement will fall short.

We have identified seven principles that are essential to a parent-school partnership. For each one, we give a range of the best practices drawn from actual schools. Some of these examples are familiar, even ordinary, but others may seem more unconventional. Some apply only to elementary schools, others to all grade levels, others only to secondary schools. We use them to illustrate how a principle has been applied in a particular setting and to give you ideas about how to implement the other principles in your school.

Basic Principles of an Effective Family-School Partnership

1. Every aspect of the school climate is open, helpful, and friendly.

Examples:
- A "Parents and Visitors are Welcome" sign is posted on the front door.

27

- There is a parent lounge in the building, with comfortable chairs, a desk and telephone, and some books and magazines about child development, parenting, and education.
- Tours and orientations are provided for new families, including those coming in at mid-semester.
- A monthly parent-teacher lunch is held in the school cafeteria.
- The principal has early morning office hours set aside each week to meet with parents. No appointment is necessary.

2. Communications with parents (whether about school policies and program or about their own children) are frequent, clear, and two-way.

Examples:
- An attractive wall calendar is published each school year and mailed to every family with information about the school calendar and holidays, in-service days, schedule, and special events. It also includes quotes of key school policies, philosophy, and a list of personnel and important telephone numbers.
- An Open House before the beginning of the school year and occasional Back-to-School Nights are held for parents to learn about the school program, meet school staff, and have an opportunity to ask questions.
- First grade teachers call every home in the first weeks of the year to introduce themselves, and to encourage the parents to visit school and call the teachers with any questions and concerns.
- Fifth grade teachers send home a "Friday Folder," enclosing all the child's marked-up work for the week and a comment/question sheet that must be signed by the parent and returned on Monday.
- A junior high principal sends a weekly sheet home to parents to update them on special events, new happenings, and sports results.

• High school teachers send their course curriculum home to parents, via the student, outlining expectations about homework, how parents can help, and how and when they can be contacted.

• High school homeroom teachers (or guidance counselors) call every student's parents in the first months of the year to review progress and to ask if they have any questions. An option for a conference is offered.

3. Parents are treated as collaborators in the educational process, with a strong complementary role to play in their children's school learning and behavior.

Examples:

• An elementary school has developed a "Learning Contract" for each student, which spells out an agreement about individualized goals and tasks. It is signed annually by parents, teachers, and the child.

• A school district requires parent-teacher conferences at least once a year for students at all grade levels.

• A high school sends warning notes home as soon as a student is in danger of failing a marking period. If the student does fail, a parent conference is required.

• Teachers at an elementary school routinely call home when a young child seems withdrawn or troubled at school to confer with the parents and get their advice on how to approach him.

• A junior high principal may ask the parents of a disruptive student to take turns coming to school for a couple of days to observe her and to help her learn to behave.

• A high school uses a volunteer phone roster to notify parents that their child is absent without an excuse. After two such absences, parents are required to accompany their child to school the next day and talk with the assistant principal.

4. Parents are encouraged, both formally and informally, to comment on school policies and (on some issues) to share in the decision making.

Examples:
• A junior high policy handbook (covering absences, grades, discipline, homework, etc.) is published, and a copy given to every new family and student. Opportunities for questions and comments are included in a tear-off sheet and encouraged at school meetings.

• A school site council (see Chapter 4, page 43), consisting of representatives from the teachers, parents, and administration, meets several times a year to decide how to spend the school's discretionary funds.

• A senior high school, struggling to develop a new policy on smoking, drinking, and drugs, establishes a broadly representative parent and community advisory group to develop a draft code. After wide circulation and discussion among the entire student and parent body, the draft is revised and adopted.

5. The school recognizes its responsibility to forge a partnership with all families in the school, not simply those most easily available. This includes parents who work outside the home, divorced parents without custody, and families of minority race and language.

Examples:
• A school principal ensures that employed parents receive advance warning of special daytime events, are offered times to meet with school teachers outside regular school hours, and works with the parent organization to make sure parents have arrangements for coping with sudden dismissal (such as snow days).

• Schools in a community with a sudden swell in its immigrant population hire Spanish- and Vietnamese-speaking community outreach staff to make home visits, speak at churches about the school and the need to become involved, and listen to the parents' concerns.

• A school district with a large number of children living

in divorced or "blended" households routinely asks noncustodial parents if they wish to be included on the school mailing list, to receive copies of report cards, and to be invited to parent-teacher conferences.

• The high school principal and assistant principals take turns personally inviting those parents whose children are not doing well to informal evening meetings to talk about the school program and the parents' concerns and questions.

6. The principal and other school administrators actively express and promote the philosophy of partnership with all families.

Examples:
• An elementary school principal fills in for teachers who are meeting with parents, hires substitute teachers for conference days, and expects teachers to meet with parents before or after school, or in the evening when necessary.

• A junior high school holds an annual banquet to honor its parent advisory group, and the principal presents awards for special accomplishments.

• A principal facilitates the parent organization, contacting students to provide babysitting for younger children at all elementary school events. The funds are taken from a school's special activity fund to which parents may contribute.

• A school district devotes one in-service training day per year to assist teachers in working with parents.

• The chairperson of the elementary school's parent advisory committee is given an office or desk near the principal's. In the high school, the principal designates an assistant principal to have brief weekly meetings with the officers of the parent organization.

7. The school encourages volunteer participation from parents and the community-at-large.

Examples:

• Each parent is expected to volunteer some time, skills, advice, or resources (money, equipment, supplies), whether during the day, or on evenings and weekends. A wide-ranging list of such volunteer opportunities (taking into account families' different resources, situations, and needs) is sent to each family in the fall for them to choose how to participate.

• Community volunteers (retired persons, students, business employees) engage in one-to-one tutoring activities with children who have some mild learning disabilities.

• Local employers offer short internship placements for high school students so that they might explore various careers.

• A junior high school, with the help of a small grant, hires a coordinator of volunteers to manage a supervised recreation program for its students after school and on weekends.

• A parent talent bank is created to provide supplementary art, music, math, and computer instruction during and after school.

• Elementary school parents operate "telephone trees" to reach parents in each grade/class to find out who can provide rides for field trips, help immigrant families adjust to the community and school, or find materials for a study project.

• An elementary school parent group organizes an information and referral service for parents who need after-school child care; a middle school parent group provides information about after school and weekend recreation activities.

The Family-School Partnership at Different Grade Levels

These examples provide only a flavor of the varied and creative ways in which some schools have developed and sustained strong parent-school partnerships. Although it can be found in elementary, middle, junior high, and senior high schools, parent involvement is generally regarded in official educational circles as a priority only in elementary schools.

With few exceptions, the publications and research that we reviewed for this guide have been concerned with parent involvement and family-school relationships in the early grades. Certainly, it is our general experience that parents are much less active in every way in school as their children grow older (see Diagram A in Chapter 1). They volunteer less, have fewer contacts with teachers, are less likely to show up at school events, and appear to be much less involved with their children's work at home.

Does this mean that parents do not have an important role to play in their child's education after ages ten to twelve? We would answer with a resounding, "NO!" Parents are as important as ever, but their role necessarily becomes different as their child grows older. Many parents of secondary school students are vitally interested in their children's schooling, but simply don't know how they should express this interest. In addition, what worked well in elementary grades is no longer appropriate to the upper grades. When parents of middle school or high school students seldom show up in school, or volunteer, or call the teachers, it does not mean they are shirking their responsibilities as parents. They may not know whom to talk with or where to go, and they may feel that their child would be embarrassed by, or even resent, their taking the initiative to contact the school. Educators and parent groups need to think creatively about what constructive roles parents can play in the adolescent years, and how schools can encourage and facilitate them.

Before we discuss this further, let us first consider why it is that teachers, administrators, parents, and students seem to be engaged in a "quiet conspiracy" to relegate parents to a more passive, shadowlike role as their children enter adolescence, and why parents in turn appear to avoid

33

contacts with secondary schools.

First, there are a number of logistical problems which make it considerably more difficult for parents and schools to collaborate and communicate beyond the elementary grades. Perhaps the most obvious of these is that once a child spends his day with a number of teachers rather than just one or two, direct communication between parents and school becomes more complicated. Parents feel, quite rightly, that no one person in the school knows their child well. Each teacher knows only a segment of a student. In addition, each teacher has to get to "know" so many more students. The guidance counselor, often the one person in a school who is supposed to monitor the academic and social progress of each child, has the impossible task of keeping track of hundreds of students.

A second, related problem is the sheer size of many public middle and senior high schools. Parents are much more likely to feel intimidated, and to get both physically and psychologically lost, when confronted with their maze-like structure.

There is also the issue of location. The majority of elementary schools are still "neighborhood" schools, within reasonably short distance from home (although this may not be the case in rural areas or desegregated urban neighborhoods). But schools for the upper grades are more likely to be further away from home and located in a strange neighborhood. (A couple of studies have cited parents' fears of the violence in these neighborhoods as reasons to avoid visiting the schools.)

The curriculum in the upper grades also appears to create a barrier between parents and school. The modern high school curriculum is so different from, and in many subjects more advanced and technical than, their own school experiences, that parents feel they are not able to discuss the content intelligently with their child, let alone the teachers. While some parents may be relieved to be rid of helping with homework, it certainly diminishes their opportunity to be involved in the academic aspects of school life.

Finally, parents of adolescent children are more likely to be in the labor force and to be divorced and a single parent. They may have less time and energy to spare for school-related activities, including the fun activities, such as weekend high school sports. Yet some observers have noted that it is often the high school athletic coach, the band leader, or the drama director who gets to know high school parents best. This relationship is often sustained for three to four years, and is more likely to be an enjoyable and nonthreatening one for parents.

There are also some important psychological dimensions to the withdrawal of parents from their teenaged children's schooling. Adolescence is a stage of transition from childhood to adulthood. One of the central tasks of adolescents is to develop autonomy, to become responsible for their own actions, and to manage and plan their own affairs independently. Naturally, teenagers start relying less on their parents and more on themselves and their peers. It is quite appropriate that parents relinquish many of their custodial tasks of earlier years. They no longer need to see that their son or daughter leaves on time for school, or make their lunch, or check their homework at the end of the day. It is quite natural, too, that a fourteen-year-old son would be embarrassed if his mother worked as an aide in the classroom, office, or library. And with her new ability to see her parents critically, a sixteen-year-old daughter may cringe when her father offers to talk to her math teacher.

As some scholars are beginning to point out, when adolescents develop more independence from their parents, this does not mean that they want to be abandoned by them. Relinquishing some control should not mean losing all interest and influence. Parents' expectations, guidance, and limit-setting are as important as ever. The period of adolescence needs to be one of a continual renegotiation of the parent-teen relationship, not a breaking off of the relationship.

While many parents of secondary school children can

continue to be involved in tutoring and volunteering in a variety of program support activities, we suggest below three critical but largely undeveloped areas in which schools should actively encourage parents to become involved at the middle and high school levels. Since there is virtually no published literature to draw on, we rely instead in this section on discussions and some anecdotal examples provided by educators and parents.

1. Continued monitoring and support of adolescents' academic progress.

It is as important in the upper grades as in the lower that parents are kept informed about their children's academic progress, and that parents show interest and have appropriately high expectations. Unfortunately, many parents have no criteria on which to base expectations or standards, and need help in understanding what is appropriate. While it may usually not be the wisest thing to help teenagers do their homework, it is as appropriate as ever for parents to insist that a place and time be set aside in the home for their child to do it.

To make communication with parents easier, some schools are successfully creating administratively smaller units within the school, maintaining continuity of counselors throughout the high school years, and creating houses or teams of teachers who stay with the child for more than one year. Some schools schedule periods when the team of teachers can regularly meet with each other and, if necessary, with the parents and student to avoid the fragmentation of a piecemeal report. Some counseling departments have created ingenious methods of collecting current information from all a child's teachers in preparation for a parent-counselor conference.

In the upper grades, it is more important than ever that the parents not only monitor but be an advocate for their child. In a large high school, students may inadvertently get lost in the bureaucratic shuffle. The schedule may become "fouled up," grades be misreported by the computer, poor guidance given about what courses to take, and not nearly enough advice offered about educational and work opportunities beyond school. Some students will be able to unscramble the confusions themselves, but parents often need to "weigh in" to set the necessary action in motion. Schools should encourage and welcome parents playing such a monitoring and advocacy role for their children.

2. Preparing for the transition to work.

One important task of the junior high and high school is to prepare children for the next stage of their lives—employment or further education. (Indeed, some social commentators have pointed out that much of what is learned in school—how to negotiate the school day, keep track of books and supplies, and prepare assignments—is all part of the "hidden agenda" of schools to prepare a cooperative labor force.)

Schools do make valiant efforts, usually through their guidance departments, to help their students explore career options, find employment, or move on to further education. But the resources of guidance departments are miniscule compared to the need; in some communities, jobs for youth are extremely scarce; and the process of choosing and applying to colleges is complex and time-consuming.

Once again, the resources of parents have been generally overlooked. This is surprising when one realizes that the world of work is so familiar to parents and that many parents have had experience with higher education. Most parents know, for example, how to apply for a job, how to succeed at an interview, and how to keep a job once employed; many know something about applying for college. Parents also have a broad exposure to the variety of jobs in the community and know where the openings are. Through the experience of older children or friends, they may have current information about a range of colleges.

Clearly, many parents are helpful to their own children in this task of choosing a career, looking for jobs, or selecting a college. But parents who become active in this

37

way do so largely on their own initiative, and not through any systematic encouragement from the school. Moreover, parents collectively are a greatly untapped resource. Parents of high school students, if asked, might be quite willing to share some of their time on a volunteer basis to come in and discuss their own job situation (as a few do), to take young students as interns for a brief period, or to act as a volunteer counselor and mentor to another person's teenager. (Teens frequently will accept advice from their peers' parents which they would reject from their own.) We have heard of a few schools experimenting in these ways. In one, the guidance department trained a roster of fifty parents to supplement their own efforts for a few hours every Saturday. And several schools are finding ways to involve the business sector in their career and guidance programs.

3. Guiding the social world of adolescents.

Junior and senior high schools cannot ignore the social dimension of their students' lives or their own responsibility to be engaged in it. While it is worth remembering that most teenagers do not lead a life of turmoil, nor engage in antisocial behavior, there still are significantly large numbers of young persons whose education is seriously affected by the consequences of their sexual activity, drinking, drug taking, and truancy. And those few who engage in disruptive, violent behavior or vandalism are inhibiting not only their own education, but others' education as well.

In recent years, a number of schools have assumed some responsibility for preventive education in these areas—usually through sex education and drug or alcohol abuse programs—and are trying, against long odds, to handle individual students with these problems in a sensible and effective way. It's a tough responsibility for educators to assume, and not surprisingly teachers often complain that it takes them away from the main business of education, and that they were not trained to be "social workers" and "therapists."

There are no simple solutions to these problems. Once

again we point out that schools should call upon parents, as individuals or a group, to help. Too often it turns out that parents are the last to know (or admit) that their teenager has a drug or drinking problem or is suspected of being sexually active or pregnant. (There are, of course, some situations of suspected parental abuse of the child when school personnel must inform governmental authorities of the situation.)

In a few school systems, principals, teachers, students, and parents have begun to put together programs designed to combat these problems. Parent peer groups are forming to work on prevention efforts such as developing communitywide standards about parties and alcohol use or, more therapeutically, to help each other with actual problems of drug abuse. They can often work to support the efforts of student peer groups. And most recently, programs are being developed in some schools to sensitize teachers, students and parents to the tragedy of teenage suicide, and to develop some preventive services for depressed teens and their families.

Overworked school counselors and faculty can not be expected to meet the counseling and treatment needs of troubled teens and their families. Schools often find it is helpful to create close liaisons with community service agencies to whom they can reliably refer students and families for help. Most useful of all is when staff from these agencies make themselves available to meet initially with the troubled student, family, and school staff in the school building to clarify the nature of the problem and overcome parent or teen denial and resistance to seeking help.

Schools have an important task to counter the "ostrich" attitude of parents who feel at a loss to guide their teenagers through the hazards of today's society. Schools can alert, educate, and mobilize parents, responsible teens, and other members of the community to try to help young people live the kind of life that would enable them to take advantage of the education program that schools offer. And schools should be ever alert to how their own policies, administrative structure, and staff behavior may get in the way of collaborating with families on these complex and sensitive issues.

CHAPTER 4

Next Steps in Strengthening the Partnership

Setting the Stage: School Based Management

We believe that a key to making the parent-school partnership work is to allow each individual school the autonomy to create a unique partnership with its community. In education jargon, this has been called "school based," or "school site" management. This is a form of school district organization that makes the individual school the unit where a significant number of decisions about the schooling of children takes place.

Most school districts now are centrally organized. This tends to create a physical, as well as a psychological, distance between the central office and the local school. Yet it is at the local school that parent/citizen concern exists, and where the teachers and principal can demonstrate that they care. All else—board of education resolutions, administrative and budget decisions, state and federal programs and regulations—has only one purpose: to facilitate what happens at the individual school.

School based management is a selectively decentralized form of organization where the power and the decisions now made by the superintendent and school board are shared with those who know and care most about the excellence of the education for students: the teachers, principal, parents and citizens, and students at each local school.

How Does It Work?

At each local school, a parent/citizen council joins with a team of teachers, students, and administrators to form a school site council. The parent/citizen council can be elected, appointed, or can draw representation from existing parent organizations.

Within carefully drawn but not oppressive limits, the school board and superintendent can delegate a significant portion of their perceived and real prerogatives to that council.

Salt Lake City has successfully implemented such councils. Their councils must act within the following guidelines:

- Recognize board policies.
- Abide by state and federal regulations.
- Stay within budget limits.
- Promote ethical practices.

What can a local school council decide? Here are some areas that are appropriate for their action:

Needs Assessment and Program Development. Comprehensive information from parents, citizens, and students is needed to establish meaningful goals for schools. The school council would be an essential vehicle for developing and analyzing this information. One part of this assessment should be a critical look at the state of school-family relations using the checklists in Chapter 7.

School communities have different traditions and goals, and schools should reflect those, as well as meet general state and district educational requirements. Student needs vary from one school to another, and will continue to do so. A regular, annual assessment of community needs, conducted by the school council, would provide a basis for establishing school program goals.

School Budgeting. School budgeting is another important

43

function for a parent/citizen council. The total school district budget is an enormously complex document. It takes months to prepare and uses all kinds of exotic language and categories that are a mystery to most educators, let alone to parents and citizens. In each school district, however, a portion of the district budget could be allocated to each school for discretionary spending—supplies, materials, books, teacher orders, and so forth. This discretionary money averages around 11 percent of the costs of running the school. Who usually makes the decisions about what is ordered and in what quantity? The teachers? The principal? Should we buy more blackboards or more construction paper? Why?

If a school district is able to free additional dollars for the school for training, curriculum study, or even for adjusting the ratio of teachers versus the number of teacher aides, these could become truly significant decisions in which the council could participate.

Staffing Patterns. The tendency in most schools is to use people the way they have always been used. The school council could be a much needed catalyst in deploying staff to meet current educational needs. It could also consider creative ways of using volunteers.

Staff Development. The public needs to be better informed regarding the need for professional leadership in schools, and should encourage its development through inservice training. The public should also have a voice in the selection of principals. School site councils are excellent means for bringing these things about.

These are but a few of the areas where a school site council could make decisions for its schools. Others might include lunchroom management and food service; building and grounds maintenance; selection of materials, texts (from approved lists, or otherwise determined), and even curriculum (although that frightens some people).

Transferring some management prerogatives to the local

school site council will not be easy. It involves trust. It is a process, not a product. Many anxieties can be created, many individuals can be threatened, and many organizational power bases can be shaken. But if more effective education is to take place, school based management, with the school site council as the working vehicle, is the best mechanism we have found to strengthen the family-school partnership.

Other Steps

Although a school based setting for managing education provides the best climate for nurturing partnership with parents and the neighboring community, there is much that can be done in almost any system. Wherever a school is wholeheartedly committed to parent participation, successful programs will be found. We say this because we believe, and the evidence shows, that parents are nearly always ready and willing (if not able). **But no matter how motivated parents are, what determines the strength and quality of parent involvement in a school is the attitudes and behavior of the school staff.**

Principals and teachers: the ball is in your court. Parents do not like to go where they do not feel welcome. In the following sections, we lay out a comprehensive process for developing parent involvement, step-by-step.* It may not be possible to undertake all this at once, so we have arranged it in a sequence. Start small, if you have to; but plan to go all the way.

---

*This section draws from a study by the Systems Development Corporation, "Involving Parents: A Handbook for Participation in Schools," Lyons, Peggy, et al., 1982.

At the Beginning

As we have emphasized throughout this book, strong positive home-school relations provide the climate in which parent involvement activities flourish. People who know and trust each other will readily collaborate. It is essential to try to reach *all parents*, not just those you would most like to collaborate with; to promote *two-way* communications, not just to send messages home; and to provide *full-time leadership* for building home-school relationships, not just to leave it to your parent organization leader.

A familiar, open climate is an essential ingredient of an effective school. Constant collaboration between parents and teachers is necessary for children to integrate the separate experiences of home and school. Families provide reinforcement and support that schools cannot operate without; schools provide services and expertise that families must have to function in modern society. Once this under-standing of mutual interdependence is established, real working relationships can develop.

Basic Procedure

The kind of roles parents should play in your school depends on what you both want and need. We recommend that you try them all. Parent involvement, like all human relationships, evolves; it cannot be decreed, and it does not happen all at once. As we suggested in earlier chapters, it grows out of parents' concern for their children and develops according to how it is nurtured by the school. Whatever form it takes, there are eight basic steps that will ensure success. We have tried to present them in a logical sequence.

1. Provide at least half-time coordination for activities.
At least one person (either at the school or, if the district is small, at the district office) should be designated the Parent

Coordinator. This person makes sure that everything that is supposed to happen actually does. A job description would include:

- information relayer
- administrator
- trainer
- social director
- recruiter

Whether a parent or a professional educator, full-time or half-time, paid or volunteer, the coordinator should have a desk, staff support, and regular hours on the job. Without this person, nothing else will go right.

2. Assess together your needs and resources.

Before a program can be designed, you must find out whether (and where) it is needed and who is available to implement it. Assessing resources determines whether enough parents, staff, and resources are available for an activity.

3. Develop a common understanding about the roles parents and staff will play.

A typical pitfall lies in assuming that everyone involved understands the scope of an activity and who is supposed to do what. Even at the risk of formalizing an easy, spontaneous relationship, it is necessary to spell out goals and responsibilities. For parent councils and advisory groups, bylaws are essential. For volunteer staff, job descriptions reduce confusion. For joint social events, lists of assignments prevent annoying overlap.

We recommend a three-step process. A subcommittee or other working group drafts a plan that is fairly detailed, giving examples of what a particular task might entail. (For example, the parent resource teacher will take over the classroom during art; the regular teacher is responsible for obtaining supplies.) The draft should be reviewed by

47

other parents and staff. Then the plan should be widely disseminated and explained so that even those indirectly affected will understand what is happening.

4. Recruit parents actively; select and assign them carefully.

Parents need to be encouraged to participate. Publicizing an activity or an opportunity to become involved is not enough. The parent coordinator should actively recruit, through teachers and other parents.

Once a group of parents has been identified, they should be evaluated for availability, enthusiasm, and skills. We recommend a screening committee that represents both parents and teachers. The parents should then be matched to the appropriate jobs. Before making an assignment final, be sure to check it out first with the parent!

5. Provide training for parents and staff.

Effective, well-planned training lies at the heart of any successful program for parent involvement. Including all who are to participate helps to develop personal relationships and to minimize confusion and conflict. We recommend pre-service training to orient and equip everyone at the outset, and then in-service training to smooth out problem areas and provide an opportunity for development. Continuous training allows adequate time to master new skills and provides an excellent means to monitor the effectiveness of the program. It also allays staff misgivings about parent inexperience.

6. Establish several communication channels and keep them open.

Parents who are closely involved in a school need to be informed about district policies and operations. Put them on the internal mailing list to receive notices and directives from "downtown." Encourage them to share this information with other parents. Include them in staff meetings, or hold periodic planning or problem-solving meetings. Rapport should be three-way—between parents and other parents, between parents and teachers, and between parents and administrators.

7. Provide continuing support services for parent activities.

In addition to the time and resources committed to a specific parent involvement program, it is important to provide some supplemental material and moral support. Not only does this make life easier for busy parents, it also recognizes the contribution they are making. Material support might include babysitting services, a free lunch at the school cafeteria, or a regular ride home. Moral support might include an awards program, a feature article in the school newsletter, or a local newspaper story.

8. Allow frequent opportunities for evaluation and feedback.

There is one important form of communication that prevailing etiquette tends to discourage, and that is criticism. Yet, improvement and growth depend upon evaluation and feedback. Specific opportunities must be provided for parents and teachers to raise questions, express concerns, and make suggestions for improvement. Setting aside time at the end of regular meetings to identify "helpful" and "hindering" items is a useful technique. Special evaluation workshops could also be held. It is helpful to frame the exercises in terms of problem solving, to keep it from becoming a gripe session, and to finish with a constructive agenda.

––––––––––––

These seem to be the major ingredients of a successful parent involvement program. You may discover others, or variants of these. Apply them systematically to each activity you undertake. It may sound like a lot of trouble, but it will be well worth it.

CHAPTER 5

Barriers to Home-School Collaboration

Forming a harmonious and productive relationship between families and schools is the most difficult and delicate task that parents and educators must perform. Parents naturally feel anxious and emotional at surrendering their children to the charge of strangers, who may have values very different from their own. Teachers worry about their professional independence and may want to get on with their jobs with as little interference from home as possible. And principals often want to establish a clear and early distinction between parents and teachers, in order to diminish confusion and conflict.

The turf battle between parents and teachers is often exacerbated by negative, inaccurate stereotypes of one another. Parents complain that teachers don't make enough effort to understand their children, that they keep parents at bay with educational jargon, and that they are more concerned with preserving their professional prerogatives than with helping kids. Teachers complain that parents don't discipline their children properly, that they make inappropriate demands of children and teachers, and that they seem unwilling to continue at home what the teacher is doing in the classroom.

Many of these complaints are justified. There are parents who can't, or won't, "let go" of their kids, who project their own frustrated ambitions on their children, or who have a narrow or distorted view of the educational process. There are other parents who neglect or abuse their children, who send them to school dirty and hungry, or who use parent-teacher conferences to discuss their own needs, rather than their children's.

51

On the other hand, there are teachers who are obsessed with their professional status and their occupational image; who are unsympathetic to parents whose background, social class, or language is different from their own; or who worry mainly about order and control in the classroom.

Most parents and teachers fall between these extremes; decent people of good will predominate in both groups. But even the minor problems they have with each other can fester because there are not enough opportunities to discuss, much less resolve, them.

Parents say:	Teachers say:
Teachers only send home bad news.	Parents don't seem interested in school.
Teachers don't make parents feel welcome.	Parents don't show up.
Teachers don't do what they say they will.	Parents promise, but they don't follow through.
Parent-teacher conferences are routine and unproductive.	Parents only pretend to understand.
Teachers teach too much by rote.	Parents do their children's work for them.
Teachers care more about discipline than teaching.	Parents worry too much about how the other kids are doing.

Other Barriers

There are also barriers to home-school collaboration that are related to logistics rather than to attitudes. These can be equally serious. One is the pressure of time. In many families, both parents must work. Many teachers themselves are working mothers or fathers. Both must make an extra effort to accommodate the other, and not waste time with trivia.

Another barrier is money. Financial pressures on low-income families are intense. Schools can sometimes help out with economic problems. Survey research indicates that many parents would work in the school as classroom aides, lunchtime monitors, hall guards, or tutors (to name a few possibilities), if a stipend were available.

A barrier common at inner-city schools, but one to which suburban schools are not immune, is safety. Parents and teachers, especially women, may be reluctant to walk to school after dark for an evening meeting. If the school parking lot or grounds are not properly lighted, there may even be a safety problem walking from a car to the school entrance. Security problems should always be considered when planning conferences, meetings, or school events. In rural areas, the distance of schools from family homes and the lack of any transportation are often barriers.

Young siblings can be a tremendous obstacle to a parent's leaving home. In many families, women are expected to prepare every meal and provide all care for the children. For evening events, schools should consider offering a low-cost meal or potluck dinner in the lunchroom and arranging child care in the school building. Or they might consider holding the event on a Saturday. For daytime conferences or meetings, elementary schools could collaborate with parents to offer child care in the kindergarten rooms; junior high and high schools could hire teenagers to watch younger children. All too often, we expect hard-pressed parents (usually mothers) to surmount these obstacles all by themselves. They need help.

Also, parents can pitch in to help each other watch the children, find rides, or fix meals, if they know one another. At a minimum, each elementary classroom or upper-school grade should compile a list of the parents' names, addresses, and telephone numbers, and send a copy to every home. Even better would be to publish a school directory. Parents

53

who know other parents feel more comfortable coming to school.

Finally, your school or school district may have policies that unwittingly discourage collaboration with families. Security precautions may require locking the doors while school is in session. Union rules may prevent the use of aides or full-time volunteers or discourage teachers working outside school hours. Closing school buildings at night may preclude evening meetings. Or it may be a lack of policy that is the problem: no regularly scheduled parent-teacher conferences, no school newsletter, no procedures for community use of school facilities. The checklists we provide in Chapter 7 can help with a thorough and intelligent review of schools and district practice.

Who's in Charge Here?

Parents usually feel that major decisions about their child's education should be made with their consultation and approval. Teachers and principals often feel that educators should make the decisions, and the parents should be informed afterwards.

This is a sensitive area in which neither side prevails all the time. It can arise over a child's assignment to a second-grade teacher, where the parents would like at least a veto over the choice, but the principal will brook no interference with a professional judgment about placement. It also often comes up around promotions or grades, where concern for the child's record is pitted against a teacher's more objective assessment.

Perhaps the most volatile occasions center around disciplinary actions. While some school districts require the parent's permission to use corporal punishment, other districts continue the practice despite determined parental opposition. In yet other districts, parents ask teachers to hit their children if they misbehave.

In many school districts, there are few avenues for a

parent to challenge a teacher's or principal's action. The only recourse may be one that is not possible or one they cannot afford: to withdraw their child to a different school. If school policy and procedures are clear and perceived as fair by parents and educators alike, many conflicts can be averted. Both sides are best served when there are fixed points for negotiation. Some districts use outside mediators to resolve the most troublesome disputes, a practice required under the federal special education law (P.L. 94-142) and successfully extended to other areas, such as discipline. Informally, principals, or school counselors may often play a mediating role in a dispute between parents and a teacher.

What cannot, of course, be mandated are feelings of mutual respect and good will despite differences. With these, both sides can understand they will lose occasionally without mortal damage to the children and to their status as parents and educators.

Whose Fault Is It if a Child Falls Behind or Fails?

There are two major factors in the learning process: student motivation and good teaching. We get into trouble when we ascribe all the responsibility for one to the family and the other to the school. It seems to be a natural human tendency to blame others when something goes wrong. It is easier to do this when we do not perceive that the responsibility is shared.

Education results from the dynamic interaction between home and school. It is not the sum of fixed parts: parents + students + teachers. No one is to blame if a child falls behind, but we are all responsible. The question is not whose fault it is, but what can we do about it together.

These tensions are a natural part of human life. It is not possible to get rid of them, any more than it is to ignore them. As long as they are recognized and dealt with openly, they will lend force to the creative interchange between families and schools.

Common Ground

Despite their basic differences, parents and teachers collaborate every day in the education of children. In fact, recent research confirms that parents, teachers, and administrators share much common ground in their opinions about the role of parents in education. Interviews with parents, teachers, and administrators show they all agree that teachers should communicate frequently with parents about what is happening in the classroom and how best to help at home, that working closely with parents is part of a teacher's job, and that teachers need more training in how to involve parents.

They also all agree that parents should enforce effective rules about homework, that parents should cooperate well with teachers and be willing to help, and that attending school functions and serving as volunteers are valuable contributions. Most important, they all recognize that parent involvement is vital to a child's success in school.

There is no consensus, however, about what kind of parent involvement is most useful. While principals and teachers favor increased parent involvement in the traditional ways (such as attending school events, chaperoning field trips, and supervising homework), a substantial majority do not view a parent role in school decisions (such as setting discipline policy, hiring teachers, or selecting textbooks) as useful or appropriate. Principals and teachers also feel that most parents are not qualified to make educational decisions.

In contrast, parents are more positive about all forms of parent involvement at school than are teachers, administrators, or even school board members. Recent research conducted by the Southwest Development Laboratory in Austin, Texas, found after extensive interviews with parents, teachers, and administrators, that parents are eager to play all roles at school, from tutor to aide to decision maker. But most professional educators consider all but the most traditional, nonthreatening roles (such as "school program supporter," or "audience at school functions") to be "unimportant." **The barrier to more parent involvement is NOT parent apathy but lack of support from professional educators.**

Another interesting finding in this research is that professional educators, while not enthusiastic about sharing authority with parents, react more favorably when it is another segment of the professional community that is to do the sharing. Teachers and principals, for example, feel that decision making is the least important role parents can play, while superintendents and school board members, who set district wide policy, rate parent decision making at the school more highly.

The Bottom Line

What is the bottom line? Almost everyone wants parents to be more involved. But both sides must give up a little to gain the larger benefit. Professionals will have to let parents into their club, and parents will have to respect the educators' expertise.

At first, new parents tend to act in nonthreatening ways, as boosters for the school, attending plays, selling tickets, and baking cakes. They also help their children at home, reinforcing what they are learning at school. But as parents become more familiar with the school staff and policies, some begin naturally to assume more responsibility and to question ways of doing things.

This point is critical. Parents do not participate without wanting to become involved. **Any effective program to involve parents will probably lead to some parent involvement in decisions**—about curricular emphasis, school programs, and discipline policy, perhaps even hiring and tenure. This is as it should be. Parents are not just extensions of their children; they are fully functioning adults who have important contributions to make. To attempt to confine their activities to bake sales and booster clubs is a tremendous waste of talent and energy—yours and theirs.

CHAPTER 6

Helpful Hints for Principals and Teachers

T he parents are the true clientele of your school. It is their children with whom you are working. Most of them care very deeply about their children and how well they are doing in your school, and whether they will succeed as adults. Parents generally want their children to do better than they have, and are willing to make many sacrifices in order to achieve that.

There are hostile and difficult parents—ones who physically and emotionally abuse their children and ones who will try to control what happens to all other children, through censorship, narrow ideologies, or rigid religious doctrine. We will discuss some ways to approach these problems later. Fortunately, these parents are in a decided minority.

To work well with parents, you will need sympathetic insight into how parents feel and an awareness of your own feelings and the impact your remarks or behavior may have on others. You also need to learn some specific skills and strategies for working with parents.

How Parents Might Feel

Parents come in all shapes and sizes. They come with every manner of education background, social grace, degree of activism or conservatism, and economic condition. Some will faithfully respond to calls or letters; others are procrastinators. Some want to be involved in significant decisions affecting the lives of their children; others would rather leave it to you. Many are frightened of school.

School can be a rather formidable place to parents, especially if their own schooling experience was grim and authoritarian. When parents return to school, they are vulnerable to all their old fears and frustrations. This is especially true when they may already be anxious about their children.

Fear does strange things to human behavior. Timidity is one manifestation. Bluff, bravado, and hostility can be others. We have all experienced the dry mouth, the flush, the accelerated heartbeat, the desire to escape. Recognizing the symptoms in ourselves can help us be sensitive to what those symptoms might look like in others. There is no sure-fire way to diffuse fear in others. Non-defensive responses, a sincere smile, and a calm demeanor are generally recognized as the best ways to build trust and reduce fear.

Why Are They Coming to School?

Curiosity is one reason parents visit schools. Parents have said, "We heard that our school is a 'Title I' (Chapter 1) school, and wanted to know what that was." Or, "My daughter is so excited about the computer room, I just had to see it for myself."

More often, however, parents come because they have been asked to come, either by the principal or by the teacher. Most of the time the request is made because their child has been in some kind of trouble. Their coming is, then, a kind of command performance; when a teacher or the principal summons them, all their fears are heightened by the need to protect their child, and by their own feelings of inadequacy. Here we have a classic "we-they," "win-lose" situation, especially if this is the first encounter with the school, or there is a history of these kinds of "requests."

Occasionally, parents come to school because they have been invited to participate in some meaningful activity, to hear praise about their children, or to discuss ways they might help. This is now a "win-win" situation, one we recommend happen frequently, so that when the other kind of request becomes necessary a great deal of the fear is gone.

For the truly unreasonable parent, there is no easy answer. It is helpful to remember that what might be perceived as unreasonableness may actually be fear and lack of trust in school people, or in institutions in general. Non-defensiveness and calm on your part can go a long way toward calming that parent down. Also, don't jump to conclusions just because the complaint makes you uncomfortable or seems "off base." A careful review of the facts may reveal that the parent is quite justified. Of course, your first obligation should be for the safety of children and staff, so if that becomes a concern, you must obviously call in the proper authorities.

There are some specific actions that can be taken to channel the energies of hostile parents in a positive direction. One of the most important is to have written guidelines and clearly defined policies. Your board of education has usually established a policy about such items as sex education, textbook selection, discipline (including corporal punishment, suspensions, and expulsions), homework, and censorship (the placement or removal of materials from classrooms or libraries). Have you asked parents to help you either adopt or modify these statements for your school? If you have, those written guidelines can go a long way toward defusing the more irrational complaints.

A second way to deal with hostile, angry parents is by requesting that they work through the school's parent organization, which represents all the parents. In fact, principals have reported to us that a strong active parent organization is the most effective way to resolve complaints and criticism of small groups of parents; its officers can also be helpful with an individual parent.

Sometimes, however, all your skills, understanding, and careful planning will not help, and a third party or the next level up in the hierarchy will have to be called in.

Tips for Principals

What are YOUR fears? Are you intimidated by your staff? Does a call or visit from someone from downtown alarm you? Do you have a clear understanding of the purpose of education and schooling? Do you have a clear idea of the goals for your school? Are you willing to share some of your decision-making powers with your staff and your community? Do you believe that you have any power?

Answers to these kinds of questions give clues about you as a person with responsibility and authority over many persons, teachers, students, and parents. If you are fearful and nontrusting of your superiors, will that fear transfer itself to your dealings with your staff? Do you keep delaying decisions and fail to take others into your decision-making processes?

We believe that the more you are able to share your daily and long-term decisions with your faculty, parents, the community, and students, the more effective your school will be, and the greater the quality of the educational experience for all the students will be.

What is the School's Message to Parents and Citizens?
Denver public schools placed welcome banners over their front doors. Some of the banners have the message in Spanish and Vietnamese, as well as English. This is an attempt to overcome some of that "fortress school" mentality which educators too often promote and which parents often believe.

Other schools have changed the signs on the doors from "TRESPASSERS WILL BE PROSECUTED" to "WELCOME. WE ARE GLAD YOU HAVE COME TO VISIT. PLEASE REPORT TO THE OFFICE." Of course, schools must protect students from outsiders, and in many cases doors need to be guarded and watched, sometimes by security guards. However, an open invitation to come in can break many barriers.

One of the worst examples we have seen of a formidable

barrier to parent participation comes from this sign on the gate of a school in Great Britain:

> "PARENTS ARE NOT ALLOWED INTO THE PLAYGROUND BEFORE SCHOOL, DURING SCHOOL HOURS, AT DINNER TIME, OR AFTER.
> "IF YOU WISH TO SEE THE HEAD TEACHER AND HAVE NOT MADE AN APPOINTMENT, YOU MUST ASK THE SCHOOL KEEPER TO MAKE AN APPOINTMENT FOR YOU. OR IF YOUR BUSINESS IS URGENT, ASK TO BE SHOWN TO THE HEAD TEACHER'S OFFICE. IF THE SCHOOL KEEPER IS NOT ABOUT, ASK TO SEE THE SECRETARY."

Do you encourage your secretary to respond pleasantly and courteously to phone calls and to school visitors? Not recognizing the presence of parents can be seen as a hostile gesture, and simply reinforces their fears and concerns. Many times parents go to a school, usually at the request of a teacher or principal, and follow the instructions on the signs by going directly to the office. Then they may stand among the bustle of the office unnoticed, waiting for someone to help them. Admittedly, this happens more often in large offices (usually middle or high schools), but the same experience can occur in smaller elementary school offices as well. Test out your welcoming committee by asking a stranger to the office staff to record the time and quality of response.

The behavior of all your staff—custodians, lunchroom aides, teachers, crossing guards, and of course you, yourself—can influence impressions about your school. How you feel about welcoming parents and citizens will be transmitted to your staff; taking the time to discuss this issue with your staff can pay large dividends in how welcome people feel when they come to your school.

Have you considered a reception area for parents, or at least a coatrack? Parents who must carry their coats while at school are receiving the subtle message that their stay at school should be brief.

What is Your Message to Individual Parents and Citizens?
When parents do come to school, perhaps feeling more welcome than they had expected, what happens when they meet with you? How do you handle yourself if they seem hostile?

A comment we hear often about educators' behavior is, "They were really defensive." Defensiveness is a response when a person feels threatened, especially when a deeply held belief, feeling, or doctrine is being challenged. When a parent says, "Mrs. Johnson slapped my child," or "Don't you think that discipline here is a little lax?" or "Your reading program just doesn't make sense," what is your reaction? Following are a couple of different responses—one defensive, the other open—to those statements.

PARENT
"Mrs. Johnson slapped my child."
PRINCIPAL (Defensive)
"Mrs. Johnson would NEVER slap a student."
"Your child must have done something really bad to have made her that angry."
"Children DO stretch the truth!"
PRINCIPAL (Open)
"Why don't you tell me what happened."

PARENT
"Don't you think that discipline here is a little lax?"
PRINCIPAL (Defensive)
"Well, you know how kids get away with murder at home, and we have to teach them everything."
"We have quieter halls than any school in the district."
PRINCIPAL (Open)
"It would help me if you could give me examples of where

65

we have been lax."

PARENT
"Your reading program just doesn't make sense."
PRINCIPAL (Defensive)
"Our reading program was given to us by the superintendent's office, and we have no choice."
"Research says that . . . "
PRINCIPAL (Open)
"Sometimes a program does not meet the needs of all children. What kind of program would you suggest your child needs?"

Another favorite response by too many principals is to blame "downtown." Everyone finds a scapegoat handy at times, yet isn't it really a "cop out" to rationalize one's inability or hesitation to make tough decisions by blaming that unseen bureaucracy? It is also a form of not-so-subtle sabotage to accuse "them," one's colleagues, of being the block to action or to progress. It is generally the case that the principal is free to run the school and to make most of the decisions that affect what happens to students.

Another favorite defense is, "It's against regulations." This is another method of placing blame elsewhere. "Elsewhere" can be the "feds," the state, the city council, the board of education, or the everpresent "downtown." Certainly, there are onerous regulations, and lots of paperwork to accompany them. You do have a legitimate complaint when a bureaucracy develops regulations and guidelines to punish the many for the sins of the few. There are also legitimate legalities that are necessary to protect children and staffs.

Killer Phrases
There are also expressions, used often without thinking, that can stop an exchange instantly. Do any of these sound familiar?

- A good idea, but . . .

- Against policy.

- All right, in theory.

- Be practical.

- Costs too much.

- Don't start anything yet.

- It needs more study.

- Let's make a survey first.

- Let's sit on it for awhile.

- That's not our problem.

- The Superintendent won't go for it.

- Too hard to administer.

- We have been doing it this way for a long time, and it works.

- Why hasn't someone suggested it before, if it's a good idea?

- Ahead of the times.

- Let's discuss it.

- Let's form a committee.

- We've never done it that way.

We invite you to keep track of the number of times you hear these phrases. Sometimes their use will be quite legitimate. Most of the time, however, they may well be a way of passing the buck, or evidence of unwillingness to make a difficult decision.

Setting Up to Win

Looking at your own behavior when meeting with parents or citizens is often the first step in beginning a "win-win" situation, rather than a "win-lose" confrontation. Of course, no matter how effective you are at trying to build that trust environment, some parents are irrational, often hostile, even before the meeting begins, and will be unreasonable, no matter what. But even if it doesn't always work, a warm and sincere welcome, perhaps coffee, and a comfortable setting can start a conference off right. (This may seem simplistic, yet we take that risk because so many parents have mentioned it.)

- Don't seat people facing the sun.
- Don't use your desk as a buffer between you and the parent.
- Don't stand while they are seated.
- Don't take any but real emergency phone calls or interruptions by a secretary.

Another suggestion is to really LISTEN. Hearing what someone else is saying, rather than planning and thinking about what you are going to say next, is essential. Also know about and be conscious of your non-verbal behavior. Are you listening with your body, as well as your mind? What does slouching or gazing out the window tell a speaker? By contrast, what does an alert posture, leaning slightly forward, and acknowledging your interest by occasional nods or smiles say to a speaker?

You aren't always going to be successful. You can increase the odds of success by doing some of the common sense things suggested. None of the above will work as well when you are tired, feeling harassed, or have an important appointment coming up. Knowing those things, and trying to accommodate to them, will make dealing with "unreasonable" parents a bit easier.

What is Your Message to Parent Groups?

Much of what was said above about dealing with individual parents applies here. Dealing with individuals is complicated enough, but when those individuals come together in a group, each with his or her own personal problems, aspirations, and hidden agendas, working well together can become more difficult.

Working with groups or as part of a group takes more skill than is generally recognized. You have an especially difficult task because you bring more information, status, and authority to the group than any other member. Therefore, your understanding and acting in accord with sound human relations principles can enable you to provide able leadership and facilitate the operation of the group.

For some of you this is elementary material. For others it may represent new ideas or concepts. If you wish to pursue these group processes further, we refer you to *One School At A Time*, NCCE's handbook on school based management (see selected references).

At this point, we take the liberty of spelling out some cautions when dealing with parent groups. (The same cautions apply when working with any group whose involvement in the decision-making process is important.)

Agenda setting. Who sets the agenda determines the degree to which people accept responsibility for the decisions reached. If it is your agenda, then you are the one who has the major stake in what is to be discussed and what is decided upon. Agenda-setting needs to be a collaborative process, with each person contributing to the items. Each person should feel free to compromise and to accommodate to the wishes of others. This does not mean, of course, that you have no substantial input into the agenda. You do have a stake in what happens and need to contribute to the creation of the agenda. Remember, however, that you have a lot of power in that parent group because of your position as principal and because you have the bureaucracy behind you. So your suggestions for agenda items will often carry a disproportionate weight, compared to those of other members of the group.

Chairing the meeting. Another area to watch is the temptation to always chair the meetings. Chairing can often guarantee that things will not get out of hand and that undesirable items will be dealt with quickly. However, natural leadership will not emerge if you chair; what people think and feel will rarely be dealt with openly if you maintain your authority by leading the sessions.

Setting the boundaries. While we feel that parents have contributions they can legitimately make in all areas of education, we understand that you may initially want to reserve some areas (such as curriculum design, hiring, or

69

tenure) for yourself and your staff. We suggest that you will prevent dissension at a later date if you are open and clear about those decisions you wish to retain yourself. Whenever possible, however, you should do all boundary setting in collaboration with parents.

Tips for Teachers

Much of what we have said about the ways principals can bridge the communication gaps between themselves and parents applies to teachers, as well. The first step is to understand that parents do care about their children, and that they bring to the school setting all of the fears and anxieties that come from their own experiences and from their perceptions of teacher and school. Joining into a partnership of trust because each of you have precisely the same goal—the best education for your child—will mitigate many of those fears, and will help both of you achieve that goal.

We suggest that you begin by looking at how people communicate, and how, through communicating effectively, parents and teachers overcome their fears and begin to trust each other. To put it simply, there are three ways to communicate—in writing, face-to-face, and by telephone.

Written communication takes time. Especially in the upper grades, where the number of students limits the number of written assignments a teacher can grade, notes to parents can be very time-consuming. If such notes become a chore, it is probably best to skip them, for grudging fulfillment of an obligation becomes very apparent to the receiver. Parents really appreciate receiving notes commending their children; they cherish notes from teachers about something special their children did in school, even after the children have long since graduated. We would hope that parents, too, would write to you about that something special you have done for their children. Most of us who were teachers still keep those special notes from parents commending us for something special we did for a student.

Increasingly, teachers and parents are communicating by telephone. This can be quite effective and very useful for employed parents, for secondary school teachers, and for those families who live in spread-out suburban or rural areas and have difficulty visiting the school. Of course, some parents do not have phones, and some do not speak English.

Many parents complain that teachers don't report problems to them soon enough. It is too late for a parent to know about a failing grade or a persistent change in behavior after those things are reflected in a report card.

When you report a problem (and it is important that the parents know about the problems as well as the successes), try to put it in such a way that elicits help from the parent, instead of making it sound as if you are blaming either the parent or the student. For example, you could say, "Mary might fail spelling this semester if she doesn't work harder!" Or you could say, "I am concerned about Mary's spelling. I believe we can help her. Can you come to see me?"

Opportunities for face-to-face communication between teacher and parents most often come through the formal parent-teacher conference, American Education Week, parent group meetings, or because something is wrong. These are rarely the best settings for open and candid sharing of information about a student. They are useful, however, if they are seen as opportunities to come to know each other and to begin to feel comfortable with one another.

The best opportunities for trust and open communication to take place are in informal, face-to-face contacts, or in joint learning experiences. Sharing a workshop experience or a training event, or working together on a committee, are all ways to get to know parents, and thus to become less fearful of them. Getting parents to participate in such events is often difficult, so you will have to find ways to provide opportunities to work together.

71

What About "Downtown" and "Significant Others"?

Several education reformers, such as John Goodlad and Theodore Sizer, have made it clear that we must reconstruct American public education one school at a time. That can be done only if the central office and the board of education ("downtown") will allow each school the discretion to make the decisions that directly affect their students.

This does not mean turning over the statutory and legal responsibility of those central office or board of education personnel. The board and staff should establish the overall purposes and goals of education for the district, determine the major policies for the efficient operation of the schools, and monitor and evaluate the effects of their activities on the students of the district. Central purchasing, personnel, budget construction, and collective bargaining are some specific activities that are more efficiently performed at the central office. But many other functions (such as tailoring the curriculum to the unique needs of a particular school's students and dealing with management problems of discipline, lunchroom, pupil safety, and needs assessment) can often be carried out at the local school, which is in the best position to decide what is in the best interest of its students.

Such sharing of decisions indicates a high level of trust in the principals, teachers, students, and parents. When there is a lack of trust, "downtown" determines what is best for each unique school, sets rules and regulations that apply to all, establishes the specifics of curriculum for all, and keeps "tabs" on everyone to see that its edicts are being followed to the letter. This creates an atmosphere of fear, and it permeates the system.

An especially strong principal or a group of teachers can sometimes make a school effective, in spite of a repressive superintendent or board; but schools can best be environments that nurture learners when the board and superintendent establish a systemwide climate of trust. Principals who are trusted tend to trust the teachers, the students, and the parents. Teachers who are trusted tend to trust their principal, their students, and parents. When "downtown" trusts its staff, there is no longer a "we-they," but a "we" in a win-win environment.

The board and superintendent also play a big role in establishing a climate conducive to the involvement of parents and citizens. For example, Don Thomas made the implementation of a system of "Shared Governance" a condition of his employment as superintendent of schools in Salt Lake City, Utah. This was a shared decision-making model, which involved all the persons concerned about the education of children, from the superintendent to parents, teachers, and students. This sent a message of trust to the schools and the school personnel, as well as to the students and the community. Such a commitment has made the Salt Lake City schools a model of involvement and trust, and achievement test scores, absentee rates, and other measures of a successful school system have all been significantly improved under the "Shared Governance" system. Other big city school systems, notably Houston and Indianapolis, have had intensive efforts to involve parents citywide.

Policy makers at the state and federal levels can also have significant impact on parent participation in the schools. Since the passage of the landmark "Elementary and Secondary Education Act" in 1965, Congress has made parent involvement mandatory in a number of federal programs, including Title I (now Chapter 1), Headstart, and P.L. 94-142 (the "Education for All Handicapped Children Act"). Sometimes these mandates may have stiffened resistance to parent involvement in districts with a fortress mentality, but in many local schools this legislation made parent involvement an important and respected part of local practice.

This underscores an important point: *While the federal government has played a positive role in making parent involvement a vital part of the education process, a commitment to involving parents must exist in the local school district for it to happen in any significant way.*

State legislatures and state departments of education also have an increasingly important role in supporting and legitimizing parent involvement in the schools. Three states, Florida, California, and South Carolina, have mandated some form of parent advisory or school site management council in all the public schools of their states. Other state departments of education and boards of education have set or supported policies that either mandate or strongly encourage local school districts to make parent-citizen involvement part of any school improvement plans.

Others who can have a significant impact on parent-citizen involvement in schooling are the faculties in colleges and departments of education. If parent-citizen involvement is made a significant part of the training of teachers and administrators, much of the resistance can be mitigated. If university personnel believe that the involvement of parents and citizens is important, their students will also have a different perspective on that involvement. State policies such as accreditation and licensing requirements can affect the curriculum of teacher training. The state of Connecticut recently made parent involvement a required subject for teacher certification.

All these policy makers and the trainers of those who make education policy are key to the creation of an atmosphere in which parent and citizen involvement is respected, honored, and trusted.

We urge teachers and administrators to encourage policy makers at all levels to take action that supports this essential aspect of school-family partnership. As we have stated earlier, we believe that when parents are involved, children go to better schools and do better in school. It takes all of us to make that happen.

CHAPTER 7
Taking Stock: Checklists for Self-Assessment

As we suggested in Chapter 3, the best way to move toward a partnership in education is by developing a school improvement program. Fueled by the Effective Schools Movement of the last few years, many school districts are becoming involved in an intensive process of school improvement. The first step in this process, usually conducted at the school building level, is a period of self-assessment.

Who should take the initiative to start a school, or a school district, moving toward partnership? Most education research documents the pivotal role of the principal in determining the style of a school. Yet, there are several possible sequences of events that could begin moving your school toward partnership with parents, and each has a different starting point.

• A principal could decide to adopt partnership as school policy, enlisting the parents to help persuade the teachers and district "higher-ups" if necessary.

• A superintendent could make partnership a district policy, provide training for school principals and teachers, and require school site councils with parent members.

• Parents could present a plan for increasing parent involvement to the principal who could then pull together a working group of teachers and parents to implement the plan.

• A local teacher center, in its work with parents of young children in the classroom, could identify the need to adopt parent involvement policies in school, enlist the principals' support, and implement the policies as a team.

• A school board, during hearings on district needs and

priorities, could find a serious lack of parent involvement in the schools, adopt a policy of partnership, and instruct the superintendent to implement it.

● A school site or parent advisory council, which embodies one type of parent involvement, could decide to put other types on its agenda and adopt an overall policy of partnership for the school.

While this list is hardly exhaustive, it does illustrate that parent involvement can come about or be increased in many ways, with many sources of instigation. The strongest effort, however, usually comes as the result of an assessment of the school's current relationships with families. The first step, then, is to do a self-study, to see where you actually are in relation to where you would like to go. Such an assessment should help you to see your strengths and weaknesses and to set priorities.

Remember, too, that the best kind of organizational change comes from within, so that those who will be most affected by the change have a part in planning and preparing for it. Wherever the impetus originates, we recommend a team approach: Form a small task force or advisory panel that includes those who must speak for and implement the changes suggested.

We also recommend starting at the local school level, if possible. Should a districtwide group be needed, form it from representatives of the school site groups. For change to benefit children and families directly, it must happen at the local school. We do not mean, of course, that district policies need not be changed, but that the process should be as "bottom-up" as can be managed.

To help with the self-study process, we have devised a few "checklists" to stimulate your thinking. We believe the checklists are essential diagnostic tools in any school improvement process. However, we also think that they could be helpful in staff development sessions and for teacher education in general. We encourage you to use them creatively; add to and modify them to meet your particular needs.

The first checklist, "Key Characteristics of Your School," is designed to help you assess your school's assets and liabilities. It covers the physical appearance of the school, the convenience of its location, its general relations with the community. All these things can encourage or inhibit parent involvement. Some cannot be changed, but all need to be taken into account. At the end of each category, we have placed a box for you to check if there is a problem in this particular area.

The second checklist, "Key Characteristics of Families in Your School," is designed to help identify the needs and differing situations of the families in your school. It covers some sensitive but important areas, such as parents' marital status, education, and employment; cultural and religious backgrounds; and child-care needs. To flag problem areas or spots that need attention, we ask at the end of the list whether any of the answers surprised you, and if so whether something should be done.

Next, we offer two checklists based on the principles of a partnership school that we identified and described in Chapter 3. These questions ask what is being done to promote real parent involvement at the classroom level (Checklist #4) and in the school as a whole (Checklist #3). What does the school climate communicate to parents and visitors? Is there two-way communication? Do parents have a chance to act as collaborators and problem solvers? Are all families being reached with equal effort? Is there active promotion of a policy of partnership?

We strongly recommend that different groups of people—parents, teachers, students, administrators, counselors, and other staff—be asked to respond to these questions and that the differences between their answers be carefully examined. Do teachers say the school has an open-door policy and the parents say not? Does the teaching staff say that collaborative mechanisms exist to solve a student's problems, and the counselors say not? Do parents say they know where to take their complaints, and the teachers say they don't? Decide together which areas need work. Then go ahead and develop a step-by-step plan of action.

Checklist #1: Key Characteristics of Your School

The appearance of your school, the neighborhood it is in, and the relations your staff has with the community all have an important effect on your school's relationship with families.

This checklist is designed to help you to assess your school's assets and liabilities. For each category, we have added an "Other." Use this space to add things we might have missed. Some of the things on this checklist you can change; others you cannot. For the really tough ones, enlist the help of your parents and community. (One school we know of had a leaky roof for years. The principal had tried in vain to get the funds to have it repaired. Finally, he invited parents to come and take pictures of the buckets on the floor, full of water from the dripping ceiling. After the pictures were sent to the local newspaper, the roof was fixed.)

Flag your problem areas by filling in the boxes following categories in which you find a lot of negative answers. The checklists that follow, based on the principles of partnership schools, will give you ideas on how to overcome your liabilities.

A. Physical characteristics of your school:
(Answer "yes" or "no")

_____ Does it look well kept?
_____ Is there an obvious entranceway?
_____ Are the grounds well tended?
_____ Is there a place for parents to park at night when they visit the school?
_____ Is the playground/recreation area well equipped and safe?

_____ Is there a library?
_____ Is there an adequate lunchroom?
Other _____

☐ Is this a problem area for you? If so, fill in this box.

B. Location of your school:
(Answer "yes" or "no")
_____ Do most of your families work within 30 minutes (by car) of the school?
_____ Do most of your families live within 10 minutes (by car) of the school?
_____ Is there adequate public transportation to and from the school?
_____ Do parents and teachers feel safe in the area around the school?
Other _____

☐ Is this a problem area? If so, fill in the box.

C. Relations of the school with the community:
(Answer "yes" or "no")
_____ Does your staff tend to have the same ethnic and social background as the families in your school?
_____ Do you consider the turnover rate of your staff high?
_____ Has there been more than one principal in the last five years?
_____ Do most of your children live in the immediate neighborhood?
_____ Have there been any significant political battles about the school in recent years?
Other _____

☐ Is this a problem area? If so, fill in the box.

D. The school facility as a resource to the community:
(Answer "yes" or "no")
_____ Is it open after school hours for visits or meetings?

_____ Is there a community playground on the school grounds?

_____ Is it available and used for community events or community education?

_____ Is it a polling place on election day?

_____ Does the school sponsor events for the community?

_____ Does it provide space for daycare or after-school care?

_____ Are school resources and equipment available for community use (e.g., sports equipment, gymnasium, costumes, laboratories)?

Other _____

☐ Is this a problem area? If so, fill in the box.

E. The school's reputation in the community:
(Answer "yes" or "no")

_____ Is it known for a strong academic program?

_____ Is it generally thought of as a "good" school?

_____ Is it free from chronic discipline problems and vandalism?

_____ Do many of the families in your attendance area use private or parochial schools?

_____ Does it offer a variety of nonacademic and extracurricular programs, both during and after school?

Other _____

☐ Is this a problem area? If so, fill in the box.

F. Special features for which the school is known:
(Check any that apply)

_____ Team teaching

_____ Open classrooms

_____ Tracking by ability or performance

_____ Smaller schools within the school

_____ Special and compensatory education programs

_____ Magnet programs

_____ Other strong programs (drama, music, sports,
arts, etc.)
Other _____

☐ Do you see this as a problem area? If so, fill in the box.

Checklist #2: Key Characteristics of Families in Your School

While a school is not a social service agency, it is still important to know the varying situations of the different families of your school.

This checklist is designed to help you identify special characteristics of your school's families, and to alert you to issues that may need priority consideration and attention. If the data are not available from registration cards or surveys, try an educated guess. (We recommend that you do NOT ask your students for this information.)

Once you have identified the special needs of your families, the following checklists should give you some ideas about how, or whether, to address them.

A. What proportion of students come from:
(Estimate %)
_____ Single-parent households
_____ Two-parent households
_____ Foster homes or institutions
_____ Nonparent households (relatives or guardians)

B. What proportion of children have ever experienced a serious disruption (separation, divorce, or death) in the family?
(Check one)
_____ Less than 25%
_____ About half
_____ The great majority

C. What is the economic/educational status of the families?

(Estimate %)

_____ Proportion below poverty level (or eligible for free lunch program)

_____ Proportion with at least one college-educated parent

_____ Proportion owning at least one automobile

_____ Proportion with telephone at home

_____ Proportion that have undergone serious economic stress within the last two years

D. What is the racial/cultural background of the families?

_____ Proportion of racial minorities (Estimate %)

_____ Number of different languages spoken by parents (and identify which ones)

_____ Proportion from cultural or religious minorities to which school should be sensitive (diet, holidays, medical issues, etc.) (Estimate %)

E. What proportion of children live in families where both parents, or the custodial parent, is employed outside the home for most of the school day?

(Check one)

_____ Less than 25%

_____ About half

_____ The great majority

F. How many children are left unsupervised for long periods before or after school?

(Check one)

_____ Less than 25%

_____ About half

_____ The great majority

G. What proportion of families is new to the community this year?
(Check one)
_____ Less than 25%
_____ About half
_____ The great majority

H. What proportion of children is handicapped or in need of special education?
(Check one)
_____ Less than 10%
_____ Less than 25%
_____ About half

How much of this information do you routinely collect? If you have not been able to answer these questions fairly easily, you may want to re-think how you collect data on your students and their families. If you use surveys or registration cards, some of the more sensitive questions may need to be made optional.

Have any of your findings surprised you? If so, you may want to consider if they indicate a special need that is not being dealt with adequately.

The next two lists are derived from the set of basic principles for a partnership school described in Chapter 3. They are diagnostic devices, with questions to clue you in on how well your school is working with parents. We do not mean to be exhaustive or definitive, but to provide a fair sampling of practices under each principle.

We hope that a school principal, teachers or school team will use this to assess the areas where the school is (or is not) working with parents, and to obtain ideas about what else can be done. To cover topics we may have missed, or that you have thought of and we have not, we have added an "Other" response at the end of each section.

We also hope that the principal will use this device to compare his or her perceptions with those of the staff and parents to get a full picture of how the school is working with parents.

Look for areas of commonality and disagreement between the school and parents, or between the principal and teachers. On a separate page, make a list of the areas you all agree need work.

Checklist #3: Assessing the Family-School Relationship

Principle #1: School Climate
(Answer "yes" or "no")

_____ Do office personnel greet parents (in person or on the phone) in a friendly, courteous way?

_____ Do posted signs warmly welcome parents and visitors?

_____ Are there directions (written or posted) for parents and visitors to find their way around the school?

_____ Is there a comfortable reception area for parents and visitors, equipped with a coatrack and information about the school?

_____ Is there an orientation program for the incoming class of students and their families?

_____ Is there a program for helping midyear transfer students and their families to settle in the school? (For example, is a staff member assigned to be their "host"?)

_____ Are there regular social occasions or events where parents and school staff can get to know each other?

_____ Does the principal have clearly posted office hours when parents and students can drop in to talk?

_____ Does the school permit parents to observe in class?

_____ Does the school have an "Open Door" policy,
where parents are welcome at any time during
the school day?
Other _____

Principle #2: Communication
(Answer "yes" or "no")

_____ Is there a school newsletter with up-to-date
information about holidays, special events, etc.

_____ Does the school send home a calendar listing
dates of parent-teacher conferences, report cards,
holiday schedules, and major events?

_____ Does the school send home a directory of key
PTA representatives and school personnel, with
phone numbers?

_____ Does the school hold annual back-to-school
nights/open houses?

_____ Does the school have a hot line for parents and
students to deal with emergencies, rumors, and
other "burning questions"?

_____ Do your policies encourage all teachers to
communicate frequently with parents about
their curriculum plans, expectations for
homework, grading policies, and how they should
help?

_____ Do parents know where to go with their
concerns, questions, and complaints?

_____ Does the principal review all the school's written
communications, including report card format
and how test results are reported, to make sure
they are respectful of a parent's adult status and
yet easy to understand?

_____ Are parents informed of their rights? This
includes access to school records, due process in
disciplinary actions, and participation in special
education decisions.
Other _____

Principle #3: Parents as Collaborators and Problem Solvers
(Answer "yes" or "no")

_____ Does the school require at least one parent/teacher conference each year for each student?

_____ Does the school offer to set up teacher-parent conferences upon request?

_____ Does the school provide in-service training or other opportunities to help teachers communicate and collaborate with parents?

_____ Is there an early warning policy where teachers consult with parents promptly if a child is falling behind or having social behavior problems?

_____ Does the school inform parents right away if a student doesn't show up for school? Are parents promptly consulted if there is a pattern of unexcused absences? (A "yes" to both parts of the question qualifies as a "yes" answer.)

_____ Does the elementary school confer with parents on the choice of classroom settings and/or teacher?

_____ Does the high school require parent approval on a student's choice of courses?

_____ Are training and resources (such as a parent advocate) provided for parents of special education students to help them participate in the Individualized Education Plan and other processes?

Other _____

Principle #4: Parents as Advisors and Decision Makers
(Answer "yes" or "no")

_____ Does the school publish and keep current a policy handbook for parents and students that covers discipline, absences, homework, dress standards, parent and student rights, etc.

87

_____ If the school needs to develop a new policy or program, is there a mechanism for obtaining parent input?

_____ Is there a parent-teacher organization that meets at least once a month?

_____ Do parents ever approach the principal on their own initiative to question general school policy or procedures, aside from situations that affect only their child?

_____ When a problem arises at the school, such as a sharp increase in vandalism or drug use or a significant decline in test scores, does the staff inform and enlist the help of parents immediately?

_____ Are there established procedures for dealing with parents' demands, especially those of a vocal minority?

Other _____

Principle #5: Outreach to All Families
(Answer "yes" or "no")

_____ Is there a policy for informing noncustodial parents about their children's performance and school events?

_____ Do teachers sometimes meet outside school hours with parents who have jobs and cannot easily get away during the working day?

_____ Does the school hold evening and weekend events for its families so that employed parents (mothers, fathers, others) can come to see the school?

_____ If there is a substantial minority language population at the school, are written communications provided in that language?

_____ Is there in-service training offered for teachers on how to deal with problems caused by divorce or separation, such as how to avoid being caught between warring parents, or the impact of family breakup on children?

_____ Are there any special programs, such as peer-group discussions, for students whose parents are separating, divorced, or deceased?

_____ Is there an outreach program for parents—especially minority groups—who do not participate at all in school events, e.g., where faculty or parent volunteers are willing to make home visits or attend church meetings to answer questions, allay fears, and explain the importance of being involved in their children's education?

_____ When a particular parent refuses to cooperate with the principal or teacher, is there a school staff member trained to intervene and work with that parent?

Other _____

Principle #6: Promoting a Philosophy of Partnership
(Answer "yes" or "no")

_____ Does the school have a written statement about partnership with parents that is clearly available, especially in all written publications?

_____ Are there in-service opportunities for training teachers to work with parents?

_____ Is time at staff meetings devoted to discussing working with parents and to reinforce teachers' efforts with parents?

_____ Are teachers encouraged to consult with the principal if they are having difficulty dealing with a parent?

_____ Does the principal offer to sit in at meetings with teachers and parents or to mediate any dispute between them?

89

_____ Does the principal substitute in the classroom or make substitutes available to allow teachers and other staff to have meetings with parents?

_____ Does the school offer assistance to help parents with babysitting, transportation, or other logistical difficulties, so that they may attend school events?

_____ Are space, resources, and staff support (e.g., reasonable access to a copying machine, typing services, a desk) provided for parents' school-related activities?

Other _____

Principle #7: Volunteer Participation
(Answer "yes" or "no")

_____ Does the school have an organized volunteer program with a coordinator (paid or volunteer)?

_____ Does the program draw from retired people, the business community, local citizens, and students, as well as parents?

_____ Is there a wide variety of jobs available for volunteers, including ones that could be done at home or on weekends?

_____ Are all parents expected to volunteer in some way during the school year?

_____ Is the program reassessed periodically, with the participation of parents, teachers, and other volunteers, to ensure that the program is meeting school needs effectively?

_____ Are local businesses and community organizations contacted to provide learning opportunities outside the school and to explore career options for high school students?

_____ Has a local business (or other institution) been asked to "adopt" your school?

Other _____

Checklist #4: Assessing the Parent-Teacher Relationship

(Answer "yes" or "no")

Principle #1: Classroom Climate

_____ Are parent observers welcome in the classroom?

_____ Are there any adult-sized chairs, besides the teacher's?

_____ Is the classroom organized so that a parent can see what happens in it easily?

_____ Are examples of every child's work displayed regularly?

_____ Is the classroom routine written down and clearly posted?

Other _____

Principle #2: Communication

_____ Are parents informed at the beginning of the year how they can reach the teacher?

_____ Does the teacher tell parents about the good things, as well as the problems?

_____ Does the teacher try to communicate at least once a month with each family (less often in high school, but regularly)?

_____ Does the teacher talk to parents in person (or on the phone), in addition to sending written messages?

_____ Does the teacher provide regular opportunities for parents to see their child's written work?

_____ Does the teacher let parents know of expectations for homework, grading policies, and how parents can help?

_____ Does the teacher let parents know what
information about the child is needed to help
teachers do a better job (e.g., family stress or
major changes in family—illness, birth, death,
divorce, etc.)
Other _____

Principle #3: Parents as Collaborators
_____ Do teachers ask parents for their advice on how
to deal with their children?
_____ Is there an early warning system for notifying
parents if a student is falling behind and/or
having social problems, so that teachers might
confer with them about the situation?
_____ Before parents are informed about a serious
problem, are other school staff consulted to gather
their perspectives on the student?
_____ Are parents encouraged to advise teachers when
a child is exhibiting a learning or school
adjustment difficulty at home?
_____ In suggesting ways that parents can help at
home, does the teacher take into account a
student's particular background and situation?
_____ Do teachers make it clear to parents that parents
must respect their need for time alone and with
their own families?
_____ Do teachers help parents understand that their
child's needs must be balanced with those of the
whole class?
Other _____

Principle #4: Parents as Advisors and Decision Makers
_____ Are parents with questions and ideas about
school policy encouraged to play an active role in
the school?
_____ Do teachers attend parent-teacher organization
meetings regularly?

———— Do teachers listen actively to parents' concerns and pass them on to the principal and/or the parent-teacher organization president?

———— Do teachers make it clear that some decisions about a child are not negotiable (e.g., grades, promotion)?

Other _____

Principle #5: Outreach to All Families

———— Are teachers adequately trained and supported in their dealings with the problems of divorced families?

———— Do teachers make special efforts to reach families from other cultures (e.g., home visits, translators)?

———— Do teachers meet outside regular school hours, if necessary, with parents who are employed?

———— Are teachers persistent in their efforts to reach parents who try to avoid coming to school?

———— Will teachers make a home visit if that is the only way to meet a parent?

Other _____

Principle #6: Volunteers

———— Do teachers use volunteers creatively (both parents and other citizens) to meet needs in the classroom?

———— Do teachers expect every parent to help in some way, and are parents offered a variety of ways to do so?

Other _____

CHAPTER 8
Recommendations for Educators, Parents and Policymakers

S chools need improvement. All the commissions, experts, and authors tell us that schools are in trouble, are no longer competitive with the rest of the industrialized world, and need top-to-bottom (or bottom-to-top) reform. There is no shortage of scapegoats: Teachers are a favorite target, but parents, teacher-training institutions, and certainly administrators and boards of education come in for their share of the blame.

We suggest that the time has come to stop blaming others and to begin the process of building the partnerships between schools, families, business and industry, labor and politicians that can enable us to make the difference in what and how young people learn. The major premise of this handbook is that the involvement of parents, of citizens, of families is critical to that partnership, and to improving the quality of the educational experience. We believe that the data presented from research and our experiences demonstrate the validity of this.

We perceive this handbook as a "Challenge to Action" for all schools and school districts; we hope that each school and each school district will conscientiously begin building or continue to nurture the partnership with families and others who have a concern about the condition of education in their community, state, and nation. We also believe that the schools must take the lead. Certainly there are parents and citizens who can provide the impetus for creating the partnership. Too often, however, when they do, it is to challenge or confront the system, rather than work for the partnership. So, we invite you, the teachers and principals, to put your energies into forming that partnership. Fami-

95

lies, parents and citizens, and students are ready to help, if you will provide the leadership.

In this guide, we have strongly emphasized what you as principal or as teacher can do to work collaboratively with parents at the school building level. This is because we know that it is what YOU do that can make the most difference to parents.

Scattered throughout are references to problems and good practices that exist because of actions taken (or not taken) at the district, state, or federal levels of education. District policies, especially, can create the basic framework that facilitates collaboration and provides the opportunities for parent-school partnerships to flourish. We also have noted how critical teacher education is to improving many aspects of family-school relationships, and how parents play a pivotal role in moving schools in a positive direction.

In conclusion, we outline below some broad recommendations for each one of these key actors in the production of education: principals, teachers, teacher educators, parents, and local, state, and federal policy makers. We hope they will all read this guide and find some useful ideas in it.

For School Principals

We recommend that principals initiate a schoolwide assessment and improvement process involving representatives of their entire school—faculty, staff, parents, and older students—to discover the quality of their school-family relations and to decide on the steps needed to improve this relationship. (You will find Exercises 1 and 2, and the four Checklists helpful.) School-family relationships may be the sole focus of this school improvement process, or it may be only one of a number of areas to be reviewed.

For Teachers

If your school is not ready for a school-wide process, don't be discouraged. There are many things teachers can do in their classroom to encourage parents to communicate and work with them more regularly. We believe that when parents work with teachers, the teachers are more effective.

You may want to try some of the ideas listed in the Checklists or examine some of the other resources in our "Selected References." Also, look around in your own school. You may find some teachers who have had more experience working actively with parents, and they may be able to share ideas with you. You may find a faculty member in your local school of education who has resources that would be helpful to you. And you may find it helpful to talk to some parents to get their feedback, discussing with them some of the things you want to begin doing.

For Teacher Educators

Teacher educators have a special responsibility to help both the teachers currently in college and those in continuing education or staff development programs to provide them with the understanding and skills necessary to build strong school-family partnerships. This includes understanding of:

- the important role of parents in education;
- the complexities, diversity, and richness of families' lives today;
- the family factors that affect children and children's problems and successes that affect families;
- the skills necessary to communicate and collaborate with parents from a variety of backgrounds and in different situations.

Some teacher educators have already developed curriculum materials and teaching methods on these topics (see "Selected References"), but not nearly enough has been done. You may want to develop your own. You will find much material, especially in Chapter 7, from which to draw.

For Parents

We have aimed this book primarily at educators, but they

97

cannot move toward a partnership without parents' help. Moreover, parents may need to insist that a family-school partnership is an urgent and important concern and to convince educators that they need to read this guide and start doing things differently. Although we have not addressed parents directly in this book, we believe they will find many ideas that they can use. If educators wish to improve parent-school relationships they must work with parents to achieve this school-by-school, district-by-district. They need parents to help them understand what they can do to involve parents more productively in their particular school. And parents need to listen and learn from the educators what parents can do (and refrain from doing) to help make the partnership work.

For School District Administrators and Board Members

Several citywide programs of parent involvement have come into being because of strong leadership at the school district level. These districts designed a program with several mandatory features and also found funding— sometimes from the local corporate sector—for the project to make it successful.

If superintendents or school board members decide more could be done to build partnerships with parents, they too should first study the issue in their schools by forming a team with their principals, some teachers, parent representatives, and board members. Using our Checklists, take a school-by-school look at how staff are presently working with parents. Decide what should be done differently and determine what district policies need to be changed or what resources need to be added to encourage parent involvement.

Some actions a district can take include

- mandating required parent-teacher conferences;
- providing the resources needed to educate parents and

teachers to use these conferences productively;

- hiring and training community-outreach workers based in the schools to work with those families who do not readily come to school and/or whose cultural background requires special efforts to be made to communicate with them;
- developing a clear districtwide policy regarding the rights of noncustodial parents to be sent progress reports and other information on their child;
- requiring some of the staff development in-service training time each year be devoted to the topic of parent-teacher collaboration;
- permitting and encouraging individual schools to invite community organizations to run after-school recreation programs, child-care programs, and study halls for both younger and older children in the building;
- leaning on local corporations to donate resources to schools, provide release time for their employees to volunteer in school, and release time for parents to attend school functions and conferences;
- developing a districtwide school calendar, daily schedule, bus schedule, and emergency policies, which are sensitive to parents' realities and balance their needs with others' needs;
- developing cooperative agreements with community service agencies to provide liaison staff to work in the secondary schools as consultants and to facilitate referrals.

For State Education Officials

There are a number of areas in which decisions at the state level can help to promote family-school partnerships. Some of the actions that can be taken at state level include:

- providing incentives for involving parents in advisory roles, either in every school or in certain demonstration

schools (as has been done in Utah, Colorado, and California, for example);
- insisting that teachers learn about how to work with parents, both in their course work and through apprenticeship in school, by setting standards for teacher accreditation (as is being done in Connecticut, for example);
- highlighting the importance of parent involvement at statewide educators' meetings and providing staff development opportunities to discuss the issues with school administrators and others;
- holding hearings in the state legislature on the issue of searching out promising practices that are already being used in the state;
- making certain that the role of parents as partners is included in school improvement efforts (as is happening in Connecticut).

For Federal Policy Makers

In the last few years, the trend in federal policy has been to move away from mandating specific forms of parent involvement in education programs. Yet a new, more constructive and facilitating federal role has not yet evolved. Both federal and state administrators have been largely content to allow local districts to develop their own strategies for parent involvement.

We have learned a few things from studies of federal programs. One is that local administrators tend to treat as important those things that federal and state administrators consider important, and that state administrators tend to follow the federal lead in deciding what to emphasize with local districts. Another is that parent involvement has generally been a low priority item. Federal and state officials, charged with implementing complex regulations such as fiscal accountability and targeting to need, have been reluctant to press the issue on parent involvement as well.

Consequently, a third finding is no surprise. Parent

involvement in federal programs has not been high, except in P.L. 94-142, where it is largely confined to decisions about one's own child.

We would make the following recommendations to federal education officials:

- Emphasize the importance of parent involvement in speeches, program guidance, informational materials, workshops, and meetings.
- Insist that requirements for parent consultation in federal programs be met. While districts are free to choose the form of consultation (advisory committees, public meetings, hearings, etc.), they are not free to choose NOT to consult. Request documentation in monitoring visits, and check with parents to see if they actually were consulted.
- Include parent involvement in all major federally funded studies, evaluation, and research. We need to know much more about how schools relate to families and which forms of parent involvement pay off in student achievement and school improvement. Make sure the findings are available to a lay audience, especially parents.
- Invite parents, advisory committee members, and representatives of parent/citizen groups to federal training and informational events. Give them enough information in advance so that they can participate knowledgeably.
- Encourage state and local administrators to use administrative funds for training parents and educators to work together. Make this clear in regulations, guidelines, and other program communications.
- Identify programs where parent involvement has had a significant effect and disseminate the best examples.
- Create more opportunities for nonprofit parent-citizen groups to provide services to other parents, through competitive grant programs or contracts.
- Be attentive to how changes in federal policy direction

101

may indirectly affect parent involvement. Shifting emphasis in bilingual education, for example, from instruction in the minority language to instruction in English may mean fewer staff who can communicate with non-English-speaking parents.

We hope this book has given you some insights and new ideas. Please come back to it on occasion, perhaps to review Chapter 2, "Basic Assumptions: What Do You Think?" to see how your thinking has developed or changed, or to share the checklists and recommendations with your colleagues. Working collaboratively with families is not only a rewarding experience, it can be a truly joyful one. We wish you well in that enterprise.

AFTERWORD

What Does the Research Say About Families and Schools?

Most educators do not need research to know that parents strongly influence their children's learning and behavior in school. Research can, however, provide an understanding of the ways families affect children's schooling and can help educators understand the implications of the family's role for their own policies and practice.

The first wave of well-known national studies examining the influence of family background on school achievement (Coleman, 1966; Jencks, 1972) were not very helpful to educators because there was little the school could do to alter parents' level of education, income, or ethnic background. However, we summarize here a number of more recent studies which seem to have direct relevance to educators' concerns. These studies have focused less on structural characteristics of families and more on the processes within families, and on parents' interaction with schools. This line of inquiry is still in its infancy, but is providing considerable new evidence of the importance of the family's role in education and is already generating some practical ideas for school personnel.

We have organized the summaries to address five key questions that interest educators:

1. What effects do families have on their children's success in school?
2. What effects does parent involvement in education have on student achievement and behavior?
3. What aspects of school organization and practice have the strongest influence on family-school relationships?

4. How have schools responded to the recent major changes in family life?

5. What are schools doing to encourage stronger family-school partnerships?

Because the research we summarize is quite large and disparate, we have relied on several reviews: Scott-Jones, 1984; Clark, 1983; Linney and Vernberg, 1983; Bauch, 1985; Henderson, 1981; and Moles, 1982. These and a number of other selected references are included as Appendix A. A number of organizations having additional reports and publications which may be useful are included as Appendix B.

Before we begin, we would like to make a few background comments about the general nature of the research.

1. Although there is a broad consensus on the importance of the family's role in education, the studies are scarce. Researchers have tended to concentrate on schools (what teachers do and what resources they have), to the neglect of families (what parents do to teach their children and encourage and support their school progress).

Most research on schools and families has examined these two worlds as if they were independent entities, largely unrelated to each other. There has been little systematic study of the ways in which schools and families influence one another and the child who daily shuttles between them. Even the many national school reform reports released over the past two years have almost totally ignored the family's role in student achievement and parent involvement in school improvement.

2. The research that has been conducted on the topic has not, on the whole, produced findings useful to educators. While there are a number of reasons for this, the most important is that the major national studies concerning family influence in education (e.g., Coleman, 1966; Jencks,

1972) have focused on associations between fixed socio-economic variables (such as race, income, and family structure), and school failure or success. Such statistical correlations do not necessarily help disentangle cause and effect. Although we have learned in the aggregate that children from poor families, and children from single parent households, are somewhat less likely to succeed in school, these studies do not help us understand why a particular child may be doing poorly or very well.

3. Three recent streams of research have taken a more inductive approach, relying more on qualitative methods such as personal interviews and observations. In contrast to the prior emphasis on static variables, they have identified variables that can be modified with positive effects.

One cluster of studies which has become known as the "effective schools" research, has examined the processes, interactions and practices that are found in effective schools. In general the key characteristics of schools where all children perform well are: strong instructional leadership, focus on basic skills, orderly school climate, high expectations of students, and frequent monitoring of pupil progress (Zerchykov, 1985). A few of these studies have included parent participation as one of the key factors essential to effective schools. (See Gauthier, 1983; and Zerchykov, 1985.) Other researchers have been investigating family processes—expectations, beliefs, attitudes, and communication patterns—to identify those which occur in families where children do well in school.

Another promising area of inquiry has examined the relationship between families and schools: to look at the pattern of communcation, contact, and mutual support between school personnel and parents, and how they influence each other. The primary purpose of what has been termed the "family-school interaction" research is to assess how family-school interactions affect children's learning and school success. The assumption here is that the efforts of schools and families are linked, that they can either support and reinforce each other or they can compete with and undermine each other.

What Effects Do Families Have on Their Children's Success in School?

The range of family factors that have been identified as affecting children's achievement in school is extremely broad: genetic endowment, family size, family structure, birth order, spacing of children, nutrition and health care, parental education and employment, patterns of family communication, parent-child activities, expectations of school performance, are ones most frequently mentioned (Scott-Jones, 1984). There has been some controversy around the relative significance of structural characteristics—those factors that are used to label families and children as "poor," "single-parent," "latch key," etc. Recent studies suggest that family process variables (how family members relate to each other) have a greater effect on achievement than do family background variables. (Linney and Vernberg, 1983.)

Family Demographics and Structural Characteristics
In the fifties and sixties a major interest was the effect of low family income on school achievement. Currently, two new questions dominate the discussion: What are the effects of living in a single parent home? and What are the effects of mothers working outside the home? Both these trends are often assumed to have a negative effect on school performance, yet the research reviews to date draw mixed conclusions.

While some recent studies have found that single-parent families are associated with lower levels of school achievement, others point out how difficult it is to separate out the combined effects of class, income, and race (Scott-Jones, 1984). Further, most of the studies lump all kinds of single-parent families together, and fail to consider other mitigat-

107

ing factors that may influence the quality of a child's life, such as the existence of extended family or other support systems.

To sum up, the research on single parenting is probably most useful to educators when it points out the dangers of stereotyping, to ascribing poor school performance to the single fact that the child's parents do not live in the same household. A more useful inquiry is What are the circumstances that allow children from single parent or low-income, minority homes to succeed? (See Clark, 1984.)

Research on the influence of maternal employment also brings out the complex dimensions of an apparently simple question. For example, the findings differ according to class and sex of child. Maternal employment appears to have a positive effect for many children from poor families, but not necessarily for children from middle income families. In some situations, boys are affected negatively, while girls are affected positively by their mother's working. (Kamerman and Hayes, 1983.) Two interesting studies have found that employed mothers spend just as much time with their children at home on school-related activities as mothers who remain at home (Medrich, 1982; and Epstein, 1983).

Again, these studies suggest that it is not useful to generalize about the effects of a mother's employment on the child's school achievement. It would be more productive in each case to inquire into the context of that employment, and the way her working is adjusted to and viewed by the members of the family.

Families as Educators
Earlier studies focused intensively on mother-child interactions, especially on the ways mothers "teach" their young children. Their findings about parental "deficits" observed in low-income families directly influenced several "early intervention" programs that encouraged and reinforced mother-child interaction in "disadvantaged" homes. These studies have been criticized for their narrow focus on

mother-as-teacher and their class bias.

A relatively new line of inquiry examines family interactions more broadly, to include the family's critical role in
socialization as well as "education," and to explore the
family's social, neighborhood, and cultural environment
(Jensen-Leichter, 1974).

These studies are still exploratory, and small-scale, not
yet generalizable to large populations. They focus on
families' use of time and space; the roles of parents, siblings
and grandparents; the effect of children on others in the
family; the difference between aspirations and expectations;
strategies of support and control; existence of informal
social supports; parents' role as mediators between the child
and society; and many other issues (Jensen-Leichter, 1974;
Scott-Jones, 1984; Clark, 1984).

One interesting group of studies points out the disconti-
nuities between the values, attitudes, expectations and
behavior of poor minority families and the middle class
values of the dominant culture enshrined in the schools.
(See Comer, 1980; Lightfoot, 1981; and Laosa, 1982.)

As a result we are beginning to understand the characteristics of successful families. Reginald Clark has identified these: clearly expressed valuation of schooling and
expectations for school achievement; parents' sense of self-
mastery and control over their lives; frequent discussions
about school and positive reinforcement of schoolwork and
interests; a family climate that has regular routines and
mealtimes and encourages a purposive use of time and
space. These are found in both single and two-parent
homes, in poor and middle-class families whose children do
well in school (Clark, 1984).

What Effects Does Parent Involvement in Schools and Education Have on Student Achievement and Behavior?

Reviews of the research have found that parent involvement of almost any kind improves student achievement, especially in minority and low-income schools (Henderson, 1981; Moles, 1982; Linney, 1983; Zerchykov, 1985). Although the findings are important, this research does have a few limitations. It is mostly confined to the earliest years of schooling and to public schools, and each study uses a different definition of involvement. Thus it is difficult to conduct comparisons across programs, or to identify the kinds of involvement activities that produced the most positive results.

Variations in Parent Involvement

Parent involvement is tremendously varied and diverse. One useful contribution of these studies is a more elaborated definition of the broad term, "parent involvement." Some have begun to classify the range of home and school-based activities in which parents participate (Zerchykov, 1985; Collins et al., 1982; Williams and Stallworth, 1983-84).

Whatever the categories chosen, a two-part distinction emerges between (a) those parent activities aimed primarily at strengthening the overall school program, and only indirectly toward helping the parent's own child (e.g., advisory, volunteering, fundraising and advocacy activities); and (b) those parent activities directly aimed at assisting one's own child (e.g., helping with homework, meeting with teachers, and attending school events). Most assessments of parent involvement have focused on these activities.

Several smaller studies provide rich descriptions of parent activities (Comer, 1980; Epstein, 1983; Lyons, 1982). They have found that the level of parent participation varies enormously from school to school, that participation of all kinds peaks in elementary school and drops off substantially at the secondary level, and that very few parents are involved in leadership or shared governance activities (Epstein, 1983). Parents and school personnel have different opinions about what parent involvement activities actually take place and which ones are desirable. Educators typically do not welcome parent involvement in advisory or governance roles, while parents indicate a strong interest in these activities (Williams and Stallworth, 1983; Docknevich, 1984; and Ahlenius, 1983).

While private schools are generally considered to have higher levels of parent participation, there are no studies to document this impression. In a first large scale attempt to quantify the level of parent involvement in Catholic high schools, researchers found that on the average one-fifth of the parents contribute substantial amounts of time to school activities, but most of it is spent fundraising and chaperoning (NCEA, 1985).

Effects in Preschool and Elementary Grades
The most positive effects of parent involvement have been documented in the preschool and elementary grades. In a review of thirty-seven such studies, the most clearly positive results occur in carefully planned early intervention programs designed to enrich the educational experiences of disadvantaged children. In follow-up studies a decade later, the children were found to be performing at higher academic and social levels than the comparison groups (Henderson, 1981). In all these programs, parent participation was a common theme, and was identified as a critical ingredient to the program's success. It seems clear that the more intensely and longer parents participated in the program, the better the children did (Linney, 1983; Henderson, 1981).

There are very few studies that have examined the effects of parent involvement at the secondary school level (Gotts and Purnell, 1985), and these tend to assume that the primary grade model of family-school relations is appropriate to the higher grade levels. If the lack of parent presence in high schools is noted it is assumed that parent involvement is not important.

One nationwide study of 20 public high schools concluded that the degree of parent and community interest in quality education was the critical factor in explaining students' achievement levels and educational aspirations (McDill, 1969). And an important recent analysis of the National Center for Education Statistics (NCES) longitudinal survey of high school students strongly suggests that high school parent involvement and support of education is critical at the secondary level: students whose parents closely monitor their academic progress *and* their general whereabouts, do significantly better in school. This relationship holds across socio-economic class. (See NCES, March 1985.)

Effects of Parent Involvement in Advocacy and Governance
The effects of parent involvement in advocacy and governance activities on student achievement have not been well documented. This is a very difficult issue to study. One review of the experience of the thousands of parent advisory councils that exist across the country found widely varying degrees of effectiveness. The key factor in their success in improving school programs lies in the attitudes and actions of the school principal (Foster, 1984). Another study of parent advisory roles in four federal education programs concurred that many had not lived up to their promise, and identified parent training as critical to a successful partnership (Lyons, 1982).

The few studies attempting to measure effects of parent participation in school governance did not find specific positive effects on the level of school achievement. Several studies have suggested, however, that where parents are involved in governance, there are also high levels of other kinds of parent involvement (Zerchykov, 1985).

What Aspects of School Organization and Practice Have the Strongest Influence on Family-School Relations?

In the last few years, several studies have attempted to understand how school policies and practices affect the interaction between families and schools. The studies range

112

from large-scale surveys of parents and educators to small exploratory studies involving interviews at a handful of schools.

For personal communication, most schools rely routinely on Back-to-School Nights, and less often on individual parent-teacher conferences. Other methods involve notes sent home, comments on homework, phone calls, home visits, and the signing of work folders. On these occasions, communication tends to be formal, one-way (from school to home) and, according to parents, too often focused on the negative (see Gotts, 1985; Docknevich, 1984, and Ahlenius, 1983). This is especially the case when the parties only get to know each other over a problem or at a time of crisis (Lightfoot, 1980; Swap, 1984).

Letters, policy documents, calendars, newsletters, and report cards sent home to all families are another form of communication. Some researchers have raised the question whether these kinds of communication are effective, and whether they ever get into the parents' hands and are understood by them.

Barriers to Collaboration

The principal barriers to effective communication and collaboration include the practical realities of lack of time, lack of transportation, distance from home, neighborhood safety, children to care for, and employers' inflexible leave policies (Tangri and Leitch, 1982; Swap, 1984; Espinosa, 1983). The research also places considerable emphasis on the attitudes and expectations of teachers and principals, particularly their labeling or blaming certain kinds of families (Lightfoot, 1981; Epstein, 1983). Educators frequently mentioned their need for more information on how to work with families, and their lack of adequate professional training on this topic. All the researchers who examined this issue recommend that more emphasis be placed on families and schools in both teacher education and in-service training (Williams and Stallworth, 1983-84; Docknevich, 1984; and Ahlenius, 1983). Few curriculum

113

models and materials seem currently to be available. (See Swap, 1983, and Berger 1981.)

Most of the school factors identified are within the power of the principal and teachers themselves to change. The few studies that examined the policy framework (Williams and Stallworth 1983/4; Docknevich, 1984; and Ahlenius, 1983) did identify state and district policies that can impede or facilitate good family-school relationships. For example, state policies can require family relations training for teachers, or provide incentives to create parent advisory councils. District policies can encourage parent-teacher conferences, set standards for dealing with divorced families, and provide in-service training on home-school relationships.

How Have Schools Responded to the Recent Major Changes in Family Life?

Many schools throughout the country are responding to changes in family life, especially to the increasing proportions of children from households where there is just one parent or both parents are employed. Yet, many single parents report that these changes are not yet sufficiently widespread. In most ways, school policy still assumes the "traditional" family norm: two parents, and mother at home (Clay, 1981).

Divorced Families and Single Parent Homes

Slowly textbooks, curricula, school policy, and teacher practices are becoming more sensitive to the fact that many children—sometimes the majority—are not living with both of their biological parents. Some schools, aware of the stress children endure during the initial stages of divorce or separation, offer counselor-led discussion groups for children in the upper elementary and secondary grades (Rofes, 1981). Yet few schools have developed clear procedures recognizing the rights of custodial parents to information and describing how to handle disputes between warring parents (Clay, 1981; Docknevich, 1984; and Ahlenius, 1983).

Employed Mothers

Most schools have begun to develop different ways to communicate and work with families where no parent is at home during the day (Ahlenius, 1983; Docknevich, 1984). Teachers are offering more flexible meeting times and using the telephone more to contact parents; some schools now routinely offer parent-teacher conferences in the evening or on Saturday.

While schools lament the fact that fewer mothers are available to assist the school during the day, some schools have responded by tapping new sources of volunteer assistance: retired persons, students, and business employees. (See Select Committee Hearing, 1984.)

School-Age Child Care

Teachers and principals have mentioned their concern about children who have no adult at home to supervise them before or after school. While educators agree that they cannot assume formal responsibility for "latchkey children," they have often helped parent and community groups develop services such as hot lines, survival training sessions and safe homes. (See Long and Long, 1983.) And increasingly, school facilities are being used by community groups to provide school-age child care (Baden et al, 1983).

What Are Schools Doing to Encourage a Stronger Family-School Partnership?

Intervention programs, such as Head Start, which were designed in part to increase the participation of a particular group of parents, have flourished for over two decades. Similarly, we now have twenty years of experience with parent participation in advisory and governance roles (Foster, 1983). Teachers and principals throughout the

115

country have also made their own efforts to work collaboratively with parents, but most of these efforts are not studied or documented. The series of studies conducted in the state of Maryland by Epstein and her colleagues, however, provide rich documentation of a number of creative and specific techniques that elementary teachers use to request and reinforce parents' assistance in home-based activities related to children's schoolwork (Epstein, 1981 and 1983). Teachers all over the country may be undertaking similar activities and practice on this topic may be far ahead of teacher training curriculum, research, and publications.

Recent Parent Involvement Efforts

It is only quite recently that parent involvement has been an integral and deliberate part of an intensive school improvement process. One of the best known of these efforts is the ten-year demonstration program in two inner-city low achieving elementary schools in New Haven, described in Comer's book *School Power*. While the program has a number of unique features, the concept of sharing power with parents and involving them in every aspect of the school program in both paid and volunteer capacities has been a critical element to its success in greatly increasing minority student achievement. Several of its central features are now being replicated in other New Haven schools.

It is worth noting that some of the recent efforts of the school effectiveness movement have also involved parents in the initial assessment and implementation of the changes. (See Fruchter, 1984; Gauthier, 1983.)

A 1981 study sponsored by NIE describes 28 home-school collaboration programs at the upper grade levels in the 24 most populous cities in the U.S. (Collins et al, 1982). The programs described involve parents in improving student performance and behavior at upper elementary and secondary school levels. The report presents a synthesis of the findings, includes a profile of each program, and describes seven programs in detail. Over half of these programs have a special emphasis on minority or disadvantaged students. Parents are contacted through individual conferences, home visits, the telephone, and workshops and classes. All the programs have strong active support of the school district leadership, parents, and every other major segment of the community. Finally, a key element in the programs' success appears to be appropriate staff training and orientation, especially in areas with large numbers of low income and racial minority families (Collins et al, 1982). The positive results reported by these programs include reduced absenteeism, higher achievement scores, improved student behavior, and restored parent confidence. However, since the study was completed, a number of these special programs have been terminated when federal funding was consolidated and reduced.

Appendix A:
Selected References

Ahlenius, Marti. *Colorado Families and Schools Project: Final Report.* Denver, CO: Colorado Congress of Parents, Teachers and Students, 1983.

Baden, Ruth, et al., *School-age Child Care.* Wellesley, MA: Wellesley College Center for Research on Women, 1983.

Bauch, Patricia (Dept. of Education, Catholic University of America) "Parent Involvement: Exploring Roles for Parents in Curriculum and School Improvement," paper presented at the annual meeting of the National Catholic Education Association, April 1985.

Becker, Henry Jay and Joyce L. Epstein, "Parent Involvement: A Survey of Teacher Practices." *The Elementary School Journal,* Vol. 83, No. 2, 1982.

Berger, Eugenia Hepworth. *Parents as Partners in Education: The School and Home Working Together.* St. Louis, MO: C.V. Mosby Co., 1981.

Bloom, Benjamin S. *All Our Children Learning: A Primer for Parents, Teachers and Other Educators.* New York, NY: McGraw Hill, 1981.

Bronfenbrenner, Urie. *The Ecology of Human Development.* Cambridge, MA: Harvard University Press, 1979.

Caputo, Edward M. "A Principal Reports: Brains-heart-courage-managing on Our Own: Six Years of School-Based Management in Key Largo Elementary School" in *Options in Learning.* New York, NY: Urban Coalition, 1977.

Cervore, Barbara and O'Leary, Kathleen. "A Conceptual Framework for Parent Involvement" in *Educational Leadership,* Nov. 1982, 40 (2), 48-49.

Clay, Phyllis L. *Single Parents and the Public Schools.* Columbia, MD: National Committee for Citizens in Education, 1981.

Clark, Reginald M. *Family Life and School Achievement: Why Poor Black Children Succeed or Fail.* Chicago, IL: University of Chicago Press, 1983.

Coleman, James S. et al. *Equality of Educational Opportunity.* Washington, D.C.: U.S. Government Printing Office, 1966.

Collins, Carter H., Oliver Moles, and Mary Cross. *The Home-School Connection: Selected Partnership Programs in Large Cities.* Cambridge, Mass: Institute for Responsive Education, 1982.

Comer, James P. *School Power: Implications of an Intervention Project.* New York, NY: The Free Press, 1980.

Docknevich, Laurie. *Connecticut Families and Schools Project: Final Report.* Hamden, CT: Connecticut League of Women Voters, 1984.

Epstein, Joyce L. and Henry J. Becker. "Teachers' Reported Practices of Parent Involvement: Problems and Possibilities." *The Elementary School Journal,* Vol. 83, No. 2, 1982.

Espinosa, R. *Work and Family Life Among Anglo, Black and Mexican American Single-Parent Families: Executive Summary.* Austin, TX: Southwest Educational Development Laboratory, 1983.

Farkas, Susan. *Taking a Family Perspective: A Principal's Guide for Working with Families of Handicapped Children.* Washington, DC: Institute for Educational Leadership, 1981.

Foster, Karen. "Parent Advisory Councils: School Partners or Handy Puppets?" in *Principal,* March 1984, pp. 27-31.

Fruchter, Norman. "The Role of Parent Participation" in *Social Policy,* Vol. 15, No. 2, 1984.

119

Gauthier, William. *Instructionally Effective Schools: A Model and a Process.* Monograph No. 1. Hartford, CT: Department of Education, State of Connecticut, 1983.

Ginsburg, Alan, et al. *Single Parents, Working Mothers and the Educational Achievement of School Children.* Journal of Sociology and Education, forthcoming.

Gotts, E.E. and R.F. Purnell. "Communications: Key to School-Home Relations." In Lezotte, L.E., Boger, R.P., and Griffore, R.T. eds. *Child Rearing in the Home and School.* New York, NY: Plenum, forthcoming.

Hayes, C.D. and S.B. Kamerman (eds.) *Children of Working Parents: Experience and Outcomes.* Washington, DC: National Academy Press, 1983.

Henderson, Anne (ed.) *The Evidence Grows: Parent Participation and Student Achievement.* Columbia, MD: National Committee for Citizens in Education, 1981.

Heyns, B. "The Influence of Parents' Work on Children's School Achievement." In Hayes and Kamerman, *Families that Work: Children in a Changing World.* Washington, DC: National Academy Press, 1982.

Home and School Institute. *Families Learning Together: At Home and in the Community: A Parenting Handbook to Build Adult Knowledge and Children's Skills.* Washington, DC: Home and School Institute, 1980.

Jencks, Christopher, et al. *Inequality.* New York, NY: Basic Books, 1972.

Kamerman, S.B. and C.D. Hayes (eds.) *Families that Work: Children in a Changing World.* Washington, DC: National Academy Press, 1982.

Laosa, Luis. "School, Occupation, Culture and Family: The Impact of Parental Schooling on the Parent-Child Relationship." *Journal of Educational Psychology.* 1982, Vol. 74, No. 6, pp. 791-827.

Leichter, Hope J. (ed.) "The Family: First Instructor and Pervasive Guide." *Teacher's College Record*, Special Issue, Vol. 76, No. 2, 1974.

Lewis, Jerry M., and John G. Looney. *The Long Struggle: Well Functioning Working Class Black Families.* NY: Brunner/ Mazel, 1983.

Lightfoot, Sara L. *Worlds Apart: The Relationship Between Families and Schools.* New York, NY: Basic Books, 1981.

Lindelow, John. "School-based Management," in *School Leadership: Handbook for Survival.* OR: University of Oregon, 1981.

Linney, J. and E. Vernberg. "Changing Patterns of Parental Employment and Family-School Relationships," in Hayes and Kamerman (eds.), *Children of Working Parents: Experiences and Outcomes.* Washington, DC: National Academy Press, 1983.

Lipsitz, Joan. *Successful Schools for Young Adolescents.* New Brunswick, NJ: Transaction Books, 1984.

Long, Tom and Lynette, Long. *The Handbook for Latchkey Children and Their Parents.* New York, N.Y.: Arbor House, 1983.

Lyons, Peggy et al., *Involving Parents: A Handbook for Participation.* Santa Monica, CA: System Development Corp., 1982.

Marburger, Carl L. *One School At A Time: School Based Management, A Process for Change.* Columbia, MD: National Committee for Citizens in Education, 1985.

Medrich, E. et al., *The Serious Business of Growing Up.* Berkeley, CA: University of California Press, 1982.

Moles, Oliver C. "Synthesis of Recent Research on Parent Participation in Children's Education." In *Educational Leadership*, November, 1982.

National Catholic Educational Association. *The Catholic High School: A National Portrait.* Washington, DC: NCEA, 1985.

National Commission on Secondary Education for Hispanics. *Make Something Happen: Hispanics and Urban High School Reform* (2 volumes), Hispanic Policy Development Project, 1001 Connecticut Ave, NW, #310, Washington, D.C. 20036.

NCCE. *Parents Organizing to Improve Schools.* Columbia, MD: National Committee for Citizens in Education, 1985.

NCCE. *Your School: How Well is It Working?* Columbia, MD: National Committee for Citizens in Education, 1983.

National P.T.A. *Looking In on Your School: A Workbook for Improving Public Education.* Chicago, IL: National PTA, 1982.

Ooms, Theodora. *The State of Families 1986.* New York, NY: Family Service America, 1986.

Rich, Dorothy. *The Forgotten Factor in School Success: The Family.* Washington, DC: Home and School Institute, 1985.

Rofes, Eric E. (ed.) *The Kids' Book of Divorce: By, For and About Kids.* Lexington, MA: Lewis Publishing Co., 1981.

Scott-Jones, Diane. "Family Influences on Cognitive Development and School Achievement," in Gordon, Edmund W. (ed.) *Review of Research in Education 11.* Washington, DC: American Education Research Association, 1984.

Seeley, David S. *Education Through Partnership: Mediating Structures and Education.* Cambridge, MA: Ballinger Publishing Co., 1981.

Select Committee on Children, Youth and Families. *Improving American Education: Roles for Parents.* Report on Committee Hearing on June 7, 1984. Washington, DC: U.S. Government Printing Office, 1984.

Sinclair, Robert (ed.). *A Two-way Street: Home-School Cooperation in Curriculum Decision Making.* Boston, MA: Institute for Responsive Education, 1980.

Southeastern Public Education Program. *Parents Can Make a Difference—At School.* Macon, GA: Southeastern Public Education Program, 1983.

Swap, Susan McAllister. *Enhancing Parent Involvement in Schools: A Manual for Parents and Teachers.* Boston, MA: Wheelock College, 1984.

Tangri, Sandra S. and M. Laurie Leitch. *Barriers to Home-School Collaboration: Two Case Studies in Junior High Schools.* Final Report. Washington, DC: Urban Institute, 1982.

Williams, D. and J. Stallworth. *Parent Involvement in Education Project.* Executive Summary of the Final Report. Austin, TX: Southwest Educational Development Laboratory, 1983/84.

Zerchykov, Ross. *A Citizen's Notebook for Effective Schools.* Boston, MA: Institute for Responsive Education, 1984.

Zakariya, S.B. "Another Look at the Children of Divorce: Summary Report of the Study of School Needs of One-Parent Children." *Principal,* September, 1982.

Appendix B:
Selected Resources

American Association of School Administrators (AASA)
1801 N. Moore Street
Arlington, VA 22209
(703) 528-0700
> AASA is the professional organization for school admini-
> strators and superintendents, has a long-standing commitment
> to parent involvement in the schools. It has published a booklet
> entitled "Parents . . . Partners in Education," available in
> Spanish as "Los Padres . . . Participantes in la Educacion," as a
> video program. The booklets are available for bulk purchase.
> Contact: Gary Marx.

American Education Research Association
Special Interest Group on Families as Educators
Southwest Education Development Laboratory
211 E. 7th Street
Austin, TX 78701
(512) 476-6861
> This is a group of education researchers who are involved with
> studies of home-school relations, family education processes,
> and community influences on family life. An occasional
> newsletter is published two or three times a year. Contact:
> David Williams.

Appalachia Educational Laboratory
1031 Quarrier Street
P.O. Box 1348
Charleston, West Virginia 25325
304-347-0440
> This laboratory's numerous research and staff development
> activities have focussed in part on improving home-school
> communications. Included in their publications is a resource
> notebook for staff developers in home-school communications.
> Write also to former director Edward E. Gotts for information
> about his papers on family/school research at the secondary
> level. 1211 7th Street, Huntington, West Virginia 25701.

Center for Early Adolescence
University of North Carolina at Chapel Hill
Suite 223, Carr Mill Mall
Carrboro, North Carolina 27510
919-966-1148
> The Center provides information and training to professionals, volunteers and policymakers who have an impact upon the lives of 10-15 year olds. Its several publications include a discussion of early adolescents' development and needs for parents; an assessment process for middle grades schools; a monograph on after-school programs. Contact: Leah Lefstein, Director.

Center on Parent Involvement
Center for Social Organization of Schools
Johns Hopkins University
3505 N. Charles Street
Baltimore, Maryland 21218
301-338-7570
> This center has conducted extensive surveys of teacher, principals and students in elementary schools throughout Maryland. Their special interest has been to identify specific teacher practices that help parents reinforce the teacher's efforts. Report and reprints of articles available. Contact: Joyce L. Epstein, Director.

Connecticut State Department of Education
The Connecticut School Effectiveness Project (K-8)
The Secondary School Development Project (9-12)
165 Capitol Avenue
Hartford, Connecticut 06106
> The Connecticut State Department of Education is sponsoring ongoing school-based improvement projects at elementary and secondary levels upon request of the individual schools. They help principals, faculty and parents examine their schools in relation to selected characteristics known to be associated with school effectiveness, *including parent involvement as one characteristic.* Based on the results of the assessment, the projects help schools develop an action plan for school and classroom improvement. Approximately fifty schools statewide have participated (through 1985). A variety of materials are avail-

125

able including assessment instruments, a report of the evaluation of the first wave of the elementary school project and a handbook on the elementary school assessment. Contact: Patrick Proctor, Coordinator, School Development Unit or William Gauthier, Chief, Bureau of School and Program Development.

Family Impact Seminar, National Center for Family Studies
Catholic University of America
Washington, DC 20064
202-635-5431
The Family Impact Seminar, established in 1976 at the Institute for Educational Leadership, aims to encourage a family perspective in the development, implementation, and evaluation of policy. It conducts family impact studies, convenes conferences and seminars, and provides information and technical assistance. Through these various activities the Seminar hopes to encourage the exchange of knowledge between scholars, human service professionals, and policymakers. The Seminar is especially interested in the implications of changing family patterns on a wide range of human services and in identifying needed changes in policy and practice that would be more supportive of family life. In 1982 the Seminar joined the National Center for Family Studies, the Catholic University of America, to become its non-partisan, non-sectarian policy research and analysis unit. Contact: Theodora Ooms, Director.

Family Matters Project
College of Human Ecology
Cornell Distribution Center
7 Research Park
Cornell University
Ithaca, New York 14850
Based on extensive research, the project has developed and field-tested three workshop series for parents and people who work with young families—"Cooperative Communication between Home and Schools," "The Employed Parent" and "Empowering Families: Home Visiting and Building Clusters." Posters, fact sheets, cassettes, activity cards and reproducible handouts are included. The emphasis of the series

is on recognition of families strengths, the diversity of family forms, family empowerment, and support for teachers.

Hispanic Policy Development Project
1001 Connecticut Ave., N.W., Suite 310
Washington, D.C. 20036
202-822-8414

HPDP is a policy analysis organization which focuses on the needs and concerns of young Hispanics. It works actively to disseminate research findings and policy recommendations on youth employment and education to community and parent groups. HPDP sponsored the National Commission on Secondary Schools for Hispanics in 1983-84 whose report, "Make Something Happen," lays strong emphasis on the importance of parent involvement in education. Contact: Ray Valdivieso.

Home and School Institute, Inc.
Special Projects Office
1201 16th Street, N.W.
Washington, D.C. 20036
202-466-3633

The Institute conducts demonstration projects, training programs and conferences designed to improve the quality of education by integrating the resources of the home, school and community. It has developed, tested and published a variety of educational materials to help teachers and parents. It places special emphasis on "home-style" learning for use by working parents and single parents. For publications list and information contact: Dorothy Rich, President.

Institute for Educational Leadership, Inc.
1001 Connecticut Avenue, N.W.
Washington, D.C. 20036
202-822-8405

The Institute for Educational Leadership, Inc. is a non-profit organization headquartered in Washington, D.C. which serves policymakers in education, government and business in a nonpartisan fashion as they make decisions affecting education. Established in 1971, IEL's work combines leadership development, networking and convening, and providing neutral ground and information for policy discussion. The Institute has

developed and supported diverse programs, including: the
Education Policy Fellowship Program, State Education Policy
Seminars in conjunction with the Education Commission of
the States, Fellows in Educational Journalism, Work/Educa-
tion Fellowship Program, Superintendent's Roundtable, Education Issues Team, and MetroLink. In addition, IEL is
associated with the Hispanic Policy Development Project.
Contact: Michael Usdan, President.

Institute for Responsive Education
605 Commonwealth Avenue
Boston, MA 02215
617-353-3309
 Affiliated with the School of Education at Boston University,
 I.R.E. conducts research, policy analysis, technical assistance
 and national conferences dedicated to improving schools
 through citizen participation. Over the past ten years it has
 published numerous reports, handbooks and other materials.
 Contact: Don Davies, Director.

Learning and Instruction Division
Office of Educational Research and Improvement
Department of Education
1200 19th Street, N.W.
Washington, D.C. 20208
202-254-5407
 Between 1979 and 1982, a special unit called Families as
 Educators funded about fifteen research projects and sponsored a conference on home-school alliances in grades 4
 through 8. The research covered family educational processes,
 the social contexts influencing family life, different family
 forms and home-school relationships. Most of these studies are
 now completed. Project abstracts, descriptions and key findings can be obtained from N.I.E. Contact: Oliver Moles.

National Association of Elementary School Principals
1615 Duke Street
Alexandria, VA 22314
703-684-3345
 The National Association of Elementary School Principals
 (NAESP) is a voluntary individual member organization of

128

approximately 22,000 elementary and middle school principals, providing conferences, publications, government relations, legal services, and other information services. It offers two series of publications helpful in building stronger relations with families. The Streamline Seminar for principals has written materials covering topics such as how to help kids cope with divorce, how to handle stress in kids, and how to deal with drug abuse. The Report to Parents series handles topics such as helping with homework, parent-teacher conferences, and selecting toys. Contact: Dennis Smith.

National Association of Secondary School Principals
1904 Association Drive
Reston, VA 22091
703-860-0200

The National Association of Secondary School Principals (NASSP) serves secondary school administrators through a monthly journal and a newsletter focusing on different issues such as discipline. NASSP also sponsors the National Honor Society and the National Association of Student Councils. The January 1980 issue of the NASSP Bulletin treats shared governance and education. Contact: Lew Armistead.

National Committee for Citizens in Education
410 Wilde Lake Village Green
Columbia, MD 21044
301-997-9300

NCCE is a private, non-profit organization devoted exclusively to improving the quality of public schools through increased public involvement. Through its information resources, which include a toll-free hot line (1-800-NETWORK), a series of jargon-free handbooks and films, a training program, and a computerized Education Clearinghouse for Parents, NCCE provides the information resources parents and citizens need to become involved in education decisions at the local level. NCCE also offers school-based management training to help parents and educators to work constructively together. Contact: Bill Rioux.

129

National Coalition for Parent Involvement in Education
119 N. Payne Street
Alexandria, VA 22314
703-683-6232

National Coalition for Parent Involvement in Education, NCPIE, is a loose-knit coalition of education organizations that collaborate in their efforts to encourage and increase parent involvement in public schools. Its steering committee has members from: National School Volunteer Program, the National Institute of Education, the National Committee for Citizens in Education, the National Community Education Association, the National Education Association, the Council of Chief State School Officers, the Institute for Responsive Education, the Illinois Department of Education, the National Association of Elementary School Principals, the National School Boards Association, and the International Reading Association. Contact: Bill de Jung.

National Coalition of Title I/Chapter 1 Parents
(National Parent Center)
1314 14th Street, N.W.
Washington, D.C. 20005
202-483-8822

This is an association of parents whose children have been served by the federal compensatory education program for the educationally disadvantaged. It holds regional and national conferences for parents and has a number of publications and a regular newsletter. "Parents in Transition" recommends some excellent publications for parents. Contact: Bob Witherspoon.

National Council of La Raza
20 F Street, N.W.
Washington, DC 20001
202-628-9600

This is a national Hispanic advocacy and technical assistance organization. It publishes materials on migrant, bi-lingual, and general education issues, many of which treat the issue of parent involvement in schools. One current project has developed policy papers and curriculum designs for five different models involving community-based education. Contact: Lori Orum.

National Forum of Catholic Parent Organizations (NFCPO)
National Catholic Education Association
1077 30th Street, N.W., Suite 100
Washington, D.C. 20007
202-293-5954

NFCPO, a department with the National Catholic Education Association, is a membership association which aims to foster parent group formation, magnify parental influence in the educational process and encourage organizations of parents to extend their rightful influence within and beyond the Catholic Church. It provides a quarterly publication, *The Catholic Parent*, and offers materials and consulting to enhance parent involvement in Catholic schools and religious education. NFCPO collaborates with the NCEA research department, the Catholic University of America and others in examining the role of parents in Catholic education. Contact: Mary Lynch Barnds, Director.

National Congress of Parents and Teachers (PTA)
1201 16th Street, N.W. #619
Washington, D.C. 20036
202-822-7878

Assists parents at the local level to work more effectively as partners with educators in making education work for their children and their community. In addition to guidelines for working with a local PTA for school boards, principals, teachers, and parents (each a separate booklet), there is also an evaluation tool for parents titled, "Looking in on Your Schools." Contact: Arnold Fege or Vickie Andrews, 700 N. Rush St., Chicago, IL 60611, 312-787-0977.

The National School Volunteer Program (NSVP)
701 N. Fairfax St. #320
Alexandria, VA 22314
703-836-4880

This is a national organization for school volunteers, organized to improve education for all children by creating partnerships between schools and communities. NSVP members are educators, community organizers, parents, business leaders, students, and retired citizens. NSVP provides a series of publications outlining helpful hints for organizing school volunteer

131

programs, "Everything you need to Know to Start a School Volunteer Program." ($3.60) Contact: Dan Merenda.

Office of Bilingual Education and Minority Language Affairs
1555 Wilson Blvd., Suite 605
Rosslyn, VA 22209
703-522-0710

Since 1980, the office funded a number of training and demonstration projects (under its discretionary grants program, Title VII, ESEA) that focus on parent involvement for those with limited English proficiency (Hispanic and others). Information about these and future projects may be obtained from: Mary T. Mahoney, Program Officer, 202-447-9228 and National Clearinghouse for Bilingual Education, 800-336-4560 and 703-522-0710.

Parents in Touch
and
Methods for Achieving Parent Partnerships (MAPP)
Indianapolis Public Schools
901 North Carrollton
Indianapolis, Indiana 40202
317-266-4134 or 800-232-MAPP

Since 1979, Parents in Touch has sponsored a variety of activities to improve home-school collaboration including: Parent-Teacher conference K-12; Dial-a-Teacher (homework hot line); Parent Focus series to encourage home-based activities; and a Parent Line (touchtone phone access to more than 150 tapes on education and social problem topics). In 1985, sponsored by a U.S. Department of Education grant, the MAPP project has identified ten exemplary parent involvement projects nationwide and will publish and disseminate a resource manual containing step-by-step procedures to implement these model projects. Contact: Alice Davis, Director of MAPP and Izona Warner, Director of Parents in Touch.

Southwest Educational Development Laboratory
211 East 7th Street
Austin, Texas 78701
512-476-6861

SEDL focuses on research, development and technical assistance to meet educational needs of their region. Several of their projects focus on family-school relations including a seven-state survey of educators and parents—The Parent Involvement in Education Project—and the Working Parents Project. Their current focus is on preparing materials to train teachers for parent involvement. Contact: David Williams (Parent Involvement Project) and Renato Espinoza (Working Parents Project).

Index

MADD. *See* Mothers Against
Drunk Driving.
Management. *See* School based
management.
Minority parent involvement, 7,
30-31
See also Non-English speaking
families.
Mothers Against Drunk Driving
(MADD), 9

National School Volunteer Program, 8
Needs assessment in schools, 43,
47
New families in schools, 85
Newsletters, 8, 54
Non-English speaking families
communications with, 88
home visits, 30
host programs, 8
parent involvement, 7

Open Houses, 6, 28
Orientations to school, 28
Outreach programs in your
school, 87-88, 93

Parent advisory councils, 10, 31,
77, 112
Parent advocates
for high school students, 36-37
for special education students,
9
Parent Coordinator, 46-47
Parent Council. *See* Parent
advisory councils; Parent
teacher organization.
Parent groups, 68-70
See also Parent advisory
councils; Parent-teacher
organization.
Parent involvement
collaborative approach, 17-25
defined, 110

educators' attitudes, 17-25, 45,
56-57
effect on student achievement,
109-112
elementary vs. secondary
schools, 11-12, 32-33, 110
moral support and recognition,
49
priorities, 13-15
"professionals only" approach,
17-25
profile, 11 (diag.), 12, 14-15
research results, 116-117
role of "others" outside of
school, 72-74
secondary schools, 32-40, 111-
112
types of, 2-15
See also Decision making in
schools; Family-school
partnership.
Parent lounge, 28
Parent support networks, 9
Parent Teacher Association, 8
Parent-teacher luncheons, 28
Parent-teacher organization
(PTO), 8
defined, xix-xx
weekly meetings with
principal, 31
Parent-teacher relationship,
assessment checklist, 91-93
Parents
as advisors, 3, 9-12, 86-87, 92-93
as audience, 3, 6-7
as collaborators, 3, 5-6, 29, 46,
86, 92
as decision makers, 3, 9-12, 29-
30, 87-88, 92-93
as educators, 108-109
as partners, 3-4
as policy makers, 29-30
as problem solvers, 3, 5-6, 87